10X
ENTREPRENEUR

10X
ENTREPRENEUR

THE FORMULA FOR EXTRAORDINARY SUCCESS

GRANT CARDONE
NEW YORK TIMES BESTSELLING AUTHOR

10X ENTREPRENEUR

Copyright © 2022 by Grant Cardone. All rights reserved.

No part of this publication may be reproduced, stored in a retrieval system, or transmitted in any form or by any means, electronic, mechanical, photocopying, recording, scanning, or otherwise, except as permitted under Section 107 or 108 of the 1976 United States Copyright Act, without written permission of the Grant Cardone, Inc.

Limit of Liability/Disclaimer of Warranty: The publisher and author have used their best efforts in preparing this book. They make no representation or warranties with respect to the accuracy or completeness of the content of this book and specifically disclaim any implied warranties of merchantability or fitness for a particular purpose.

The advice and strategies contained herein may not be suitable for your situation. You should consult with a professional where appropriate. All income examples are just that, examples. They are not intended to represent or guarantee that everyone will achieve similar results. Neither the publisher nor author shall be liable for any loss of profit or any other commercial damages, including but not limited to special, incidental, consequential, or other damages.

For bulk copies of this book, general information on other Grant Cardone products and services, or for technical support, please contact Cardone Training Technologies, Inc., 310-777-0255.

Publishing services by Niche Pressworks, Indianapolis, IN

Library of Congress Control Number: 2022908198
ISBN: 978-1-945661-60-0 (Paperback edition)
ISBN: 978-1-945661-61-7 (eBook edition)

Printed in the United States of America

CONTENTS

If You're an Entrepreneur ... You Need to Read This · · · · · · · · ix

1 The 10X Rule · 1
   What Is the 10X Mindset?   5
   What Is 10X Action?   7

2 Average Is a Failing Formula · 13
   10X Mindset: It's as Easy to Think Big as It Is
     to Think Small   17
   10X Action: Think Big, Then Share the Vision   19

3 Fear Is a Liar · 25
   10X Mindset: Fear Is Not Based on Rational Thought   29
   10X Action: Let Fear Guide You   31

4 Dominate, Don't Compete · 37
   10X Mindset: Pursue Domination   40
   10X Action: Seek Your Unfair Advantage   42

5 Obsession Is a Gift · 47
   10X Mindset: Choose Your Obsessions   51
   10X Action: Four Degrees of Action   53

6 Expand, Don't Contract · 59
   10X Mindset: Take 100 Percent Responsibility   63
   10X Action: Go in the Opposite Direction of the Market   65

7	**Leveraging Your Resources** ·71
	10X Mindset: Use It or Lose It 74
	10X Action: Multiply Your Assets 76
8	**Omnipresence** · 81
	10X Mindset: Saturation, Not Satisfaction 84
	10X Action: Be Omnipresent 86
9	**Burn It Down or Burn Out** · 91
	10X Mindset: Commit to Your Purpose 94
	10X Action: Get the Lighter Fluid 96
10	**Excuse-Free Living *(a.k.a., "Don't Be a Victim")*** · · · · · · · · 101
	10X Mindset: Success Is Mandatory 104
	10X Action: Commit to an Excuse-Free Life 106

Getting Started with 10X · 111
    10X Mindset: Embrace the Path   114
    10X Action: Choose Who Is Allowed to Speak
        into Your Life   116

About Grant Cardone · 121

OTHER BOOKS BY GRANT CARDONE

The 10X Rule
Sell or Be Sold
How to Create Wealth Investing in Real Estate
The Millionaire Booklet
If You're Not First, You're Last
The Closer's Survival Guide
Grant Cardone's PlayBook to Millions
10X Kids
10X Sales Pro
The 10X Mentor (Audible)

> "Playing small is not a survival strategy."
>
> – GC

10X

INTRODUCTION

IF YOU'RE AN ENTREPRENEUR ... YOU NEED TO READ THIS

There is a huge opportunity bubbling up in the next few years. Like a wave gathering itself before crashing to the shore, certain sectors are experiencing a rumbling that will precede an incredible transfer of wealth.

Ten trillion dollars — yes, TRILLION — in assets will change hands in less than a decade.[1] Business owners are retiring, shutting down, going out of business ... leaving a vacuum in their wake.

And we all know what nature does with a vacuum!

Something and someone will rush in to take the place of the disappearing dry cleaner, the retiring auto mechanic, or the pizza joint that closed during COVID and never reopened.

So, the question becomes ... Will you be one of the ones to reap the spoils of this unprecedented time in our history?

Because you've read this far, I'd bet money that you're better prepared than most entrepreneurs to do just that. Look, I talk to a lot of business owners day in and day out, and the ones who think they know it all are usually those who don't have a clue, while those who are humble and hungry enough to say, "Teach me!" are usually way ahead of the game. Congrats on being in the latter group. You've already taken a stand for excellence.

10X Entrepreneur is a companion to my bestselling book, *The 10X Rule: The Only Difference Between Success and Failure*. You do not need to have read *The 10X Rule* to catch what I'm laying down in this book, so keep reading. However, *The 10X Rule* is a bestseller for a reason. It contains unique perspectives, valuable guidance, and unconventional wisdom for creating and maintaining 10X Success in every area of your life.

When I think back to over a decade ago when I wrote *The 10X Rule*, the world was in a very different state. The United States was emerging from what many thought would be the toughest economic situation we'd see in our lifetime. No one saw what the future would bring: a global pandemic, international unrest, massive challenges to the worldwide supply chain, political upheaval, and more.

That's one main reason why *10X Entrepreneur* is needed right now. While the basic principles of the 10X Rule are eternal, the world is a much more volatile place. Many businesses (and individuals) have yet to fully recover economically, politically, and emotionally from the past few years. I wanted to provide a guide for how anyone, particularly entrepreneurs, can use the 10X approach to deal with constant uncertainty — and to make money from the opportunities presented in times of change.

Entrepreneurs are used to forging new paths, but today's economic environment is likely something no one has ever experienced before. Yes, it presents unprecedented opportunity — but it also presents unprecedented challenges, ones you may feel ill-equipped to handle.

Despite the challenges and hardships, I believe entrepreneurs will be the saviors of this country. There's something about our mental and emotional makeup that means hard times call out the best in us. While others in our culture have simply given up (see the number of people who have simply refused to reenter the workforce, for example), entrepreneurs are the ones who will rise to the challenges before us and bring value, service, and hope to the world.

ENTREPRENEUR (noun)
"a person who organizes and operates a business or businesses, taking on greater than normal financial risks in order to do so."[2]

If you move forward with the right attitude and the right actions (both of which I will show you in this book), you cannot lose. Now is the time to see what you are really made of and test the edges of your self-imposed limitations — and that's what the 10X Rule is all about.

At its most basic, the 10X Rule is the single principle that all top achievers adhere to — in any arena. Regardless of how you personally define "success," the 10X Rule will help you attain it, despite a poor economy, personal hardship, education (or lack thereof), or any other objection.

The 10X Rule is what I attribute my own success to, and in this book, I will show you how to use it to reach unimaginable levels of personal and sales success. I'll help you define the correct goals, accurately estimate the effort required to reach those goals, and keep the necessary mindset to consistently execute against those goals.

Whether you're new to business ownership or you're a serial entrepreneur ...

Starting your first business or your 50th ...

Trying to turn around a struggling business or ready to expand ...

Selling products, services, consulting, or donuts ...

... If you are an entrepreneur, this book is for you.

After three decades of entrepreneurship, I've learned a thing or two. I'll show you everything I know because that is my mission: to equip people just like you to help change the world.

Let's get to work!

– GC

ENTREPRENEURIAL STATISTICS YOU NEED TO KNOW

Be proud of being a business owner. Entrepreneurs fuel the world:

- There are over 90 million entrepreneurs in the US.[3]
- 83.1% of US business owners started, as opposed to purchased, their companies.[4]
- In 2015, small business employment comprised about 45% of total private employment in the US.[5]
- The average entrepreneur makes about $86,943 per year (but who wants to be average???).[6]

> **"10X the goals, 10X the action, and you'll get everything you ever dreamed of."**
>
> — GC

CHAPTER 1

THE 10X RULE

It's been said that the best course in personal development is being an entrepreneur because when you're on the line for the success or failure of your business, all your flaws and shortcomings as an individual are put in the spotlight. There's nowhere to run when it's 11:59 p.m. the day before payroll, and you have no idea where the cash is going to come from.

I fully agree.

Nothing has forced me to expand my capabilities, leadership ability, vision, and character more than the three decades I've spent as an entrepreneur and business owner.

If you look at my life now, you may think I've always been the handsome, successful devil you see in front of you, with the Malibu beach house, the gorgeous and talented wife, the adorable, intelligent kids, the multiple businesses generating over $100 million in annual revenue, the helicopters, the jet, and the millions of social media followers.

You may wonder what I could possibly teach you about owning and scaling a business when it's obvious I was born into the lap of luxury, complete with box seats to the Saints and a platinum AmEx card.

If that's what you think of me, you're dead wrong. I am truly a rags-to-riches story with the bumps and stitches and scars to show for my mistakes along the way. I've covered my story in detail in other books, but I wanted to share the basics here, so you know my path hasn't been strewn with rose petals.

The short story: Until I was 10, I had a pretty normal childhood in Lake Charles, Louisiana. We pinched our pennies like most families with five children, but I was a pretty typical, hyper kid. Then one day, my dad died.

Boom.

Within a matter of days, our house was on the market, and we were hit in the face with our new reality of not having a father in our home. My mom did her best to hold it all together for us, but with no real education and no work experience, her options for making money were limited.

As you can imagine, I was not okay with this series of events. I was basically driven by anger. Combine that with my energy level and I was simply looking for trouble — and I found it. I told everyone who would listen that someday I'd be rich. Really rich. Big-time rich. Never-worry-about-using-too-much-toilet-paper rich. They laughed, and I don't blame 'em. I was a mess.

Flash forward to my early 20s. I had an anger problem, a sales job I hated, and a drug addiction. The drugs put me in proximity to some unsavory characters. One gave me a beating so bad I ended up in the hospital with 75 stitches in my head.

I still didn't give up the drugs. Talk about hardheaded!

Finally, my mom told me to make a choice: I could keep using, but if I did, I couldn't keep coming around. That broke through the haze, and I entered rehab for exactly 29 days. I wasn't ready to leave at that point, but my insurance had run out, so they showed me the door.

Two things came out of that stay. First, I learned that I could stay off drugs for 29 days. Second, they pissed me off. My "counselor" told me I'd never amount to anything more than being an addict. If I was lucky and focused on it, I'd stay clean. But I should give up on my dreams of riches.

I had one answer: Bullshit. I was gonna prove this jerk wrong if it was the last thing I did.

(We'll talk more about "haters" later ... But let me say right now, treat anyone who puts down your goals and dreams like poison because that's what they are.)

I committed to not only staying away from alcohol and drugs, but also to turning my obsessive personality into an asset. *I would become obsessed with success.*

I had no idea what that meant, other than it was basically the opposite of how I'd been living. So I did the only thing I knew how to do and started right where I was.

I hated my job in car sales, but it was what I had, so I chose to throw myself into it. I would take all the energy that I'd been putting into my drug addiction and redirect it toward my career. It was there that I realized that the bigger the goals I set and the harder I worked to make them happen, the more success I realized. That was the beginning of the 10X Rule.

Over time, my results grew. Within a matter of years, I was in the top one percent of salespeople in the entire auto industry. Other salespeople — after they got done mocking me and criticizing my efforts — started asking me how I was doing it. Informal mentoring led to more formal sales training, and I eventually launched my sales training and consulting business in 1987.

The important thing I want you to take away is that during the times in my life when things were going well, I was setting massive goals and taking massive action, period. Instead of fighting against my obsessive personality, I began to channel it in a positive direction.

This became my path to success.

SUCCESS (noun)

"degree or measure of succeeding, or favorable or desired outcome."[7]

Like most things viewed in the rearview mirror, my path looks straight and inevitable. But I was also plagued with the uncertainties, challenges, and rejection that every entrepreneur experiences. You'll hear more about those stories throughout this book.

No matter what I desired — personal finances with indestructible wealth, a lasting business legacy, one million customers — all I had to do was keep setting big goals (10 times higher than I thought I needed to set them) and then do 10 times more than what I thought would be necessary to achieve those goals.

This is the formula: **10X Mindset + 10X Action = 10X Success**

This formula is the one single thing that has made the biggest difference in my business and personal life as well as in the lives of hundreds of thousands of other business owners and entrepreneurs. Don't let its simplicity fool you. I promise that once you internalize it, your life will change dramatically for the better.

In the rest of this chapter, I'm going to break this very simple formula down even further so you understand *exactly* what I mean by 10X Mindset and 10X Action.

In the rest of the book, I'll introduce you to some important elements of the 10X Rule, showing you how they apply to business owners like you, and how you can use them to confront and overcome typical entrepreneurial challenges. Get ready for lots of stories and examples so you can see the 10X Formula in action.

Okay, let's do this ...

WHAT IS THE 10X MINDSET?

You became an entrepreneur because you dream of a better world. Whether it's a better mousetrap, a better pool installation business, a better app for tracking expenses, or a better sales training company, you have an idea to improve the lives of your customers and clients.

That's why I know you're never gonna be satisfied with *average*.

While the rest of the world settles for average — average income, average relationships, average health, average families — not me. And not YOU.

The key to growing your business to unfathomable levels is to adjust your thinking. It all starts in the mind. Before you can reach extraordinary results, you have to set extraordinary goals. You have to see it in your mind before you can achieve it.

See if this story sounds familiar:

Roberto owns a commercial cleaning service and employs 10 people. His average monthly gross revenue is $45,000. After seeing a GC video on TikTok, he's ready to go all in. This is gonna be his year! That Grant Cardone brother is nuts, though. But Roberto knows he can do better, so he aims to hit $60,000 a month this year. That's reasonable.

The first month out, Roberto hits up all his old service contracts and lands a few. He thinks he's off to a great start at $52,000.

In month two, he adds a few accounts but loses a few contracts that either don't renew or reduce their schedules. A lot of people are working from home now, and businesses just don't need the same level of service. He's slightly up from last year at $49,000. Thankfully, last month was good.

Month three hits and Roberto sees a bunch of reports about how slow things are in commercial real estate. Vacancies are sky-high. "Wow," he tells himself. "Forget about expanding. We're lucky to be holding steady!" He's happy to do $40,000 this month.

The next few months are more of the same. Some are up a bit; some are down. The news is bad everywhere. He knows a couple of competitors who are laying off workers. He'll just lay low, offer some discounts to get customers to sign for another year, and try to make it through.

And so the rest of the year goes, with the average for the year coming in at $44,000 — down from the previous year, but he's just happy to still be in business. Next year will be better, right?

Here's the problem. By aiming for marginal growth (33 percent), Roberto thought he could achieve his goals with a marginal increase in effort. He didn't have to fundamentally change anything about the way he was doing business. It was just hitting the gas a little bit harder.

But what if he had 10Xed his goal? What if he'd bought into the vision and said, "This is it. I'm tired of playing small. I'm gonna do whatever it takes to make this a $5 million business"?

He would have had to adopt a totally different approach to his business. His mindset would have shifted dramatically. What got Roberto to $45,000 a month won't get him to $450,000. He would have had to rip his business apart at the foundations and rebuild in a completely different manner. He would have had to innovate, trying things no one else in his industry was even thinking about. Sure, some ideas would have fallen flat or even lost him a bit of money. But some would have paid off. And maybe Roberto wouldn't have hit $5.4 million for the year, but he sure as heck wouldn't have gone *backward*.

Roberto needed to get out of his comfort zone and into unknown territory. That's what a 10X Mindset forces. And new ways of thinking lead to new levels of success … when you back that thought up with 10X Action.

WHAT IS 10X ACTION?

There's a phrase I learned from a Texan buddy of mine: "That guy is all hat, no cattle."

In other words, he says all the right stuff but never backs it up. It's the dude who struts around the gym, giving everyone else advice and bragging about his keto diet goals and his lifting plan. But the next time you see him, he looks exactly the same. All talk, no action.

These people may actually believe what they say, but they can't seem to follow up their big talk with big action, so their plans fall flat. The entrepreneurial world is full of people who have the next big idea but never go beyond the planning stage.

Do you think Elon Musk was the first guy to think about building a better electric car or going to Mars? Not even close. But he's the first one to take concrete action — massive action — toward achieving those goals. As a result, he's now the world's richest man (at least until I catch up!).

Setting big goals is the first step to 10X Success. It's necessary, but it's not sufficient. Action — specifically 10X Action — must follow.

Massive 10X Action is your secret weapon. It will give you a leg up against those in your industry who are better funded, who have a larger customer base, or who have a head start to market.

When I was establishing my sales training company, I wasn't smarter than my competitors. I didn't have a Rolodex full of contacts. I had no family connections. I had limited funds. But I was obsessed (10X Mindset), and I was willing to outwork anyone (10X Action).

Every success in my life, from winning over my wife to appearing on *Undercover Billionaire* and building a multi-million-dollar business in just 90 days, came about not only because I had the vision, but because I put forth a minimum of 10 times the amount of action I anticipated that would be necessary to achieve my goals.

10X Action is critical to your 10X Success.

The biggest mistake you can make when launching and scaling your business is severely underestimating the actions, resources, money, and energy it will take to reach your goals.

Ask any entrepreneur, from Spanx founder Sara Blakely to the kid selling lemonade on the corner. The path to success will take significantly longer — and cost significantly more — than you anticipate. Always. And if you're not prepared for the setbacks and delays, you will get discouraged, frustrated, and bitter.

You want to have 10,000 paid installs of your new software by year-end? You better 10X that and aim for 100,000 users because you're gonna have to deal with:

- Tech bugs and delays
- Employee turnover
- Customer service issues
- Funding problems
- "Me too" imitators (including that key software developer who jumps ship and starts a similar business)
- Legal challenges
- And more …

If you aren't prepared for these obstacles, you're in for a harsh reality check. Try standing up in front of the company at an all-hands meeting and trying to stay positive when you've overdrawn your bank account, and the software program is three months behind schedule.

Successful entrepreneurs know there's a balance between realism and pessimism. Things rarely go according to plan. Funders back out, employees and customers sue you, and illnesses hit at the least favorable time. But 10X Action insulates you against the ups and downs because you were expecting them all along on your road to success.

CHAPTER RECAP

- Most people are content with "average." If you want more than average, you have to think bigger and take more action.
- The 10X Formula:
  10X Mindset + 10X Action = 10X Success
- 10X Mindset forces you to think outside the box.
- 10X Action provides a cushion against setbacks and problems that are bound to occur.

HOW LONG??

Facebook didn't make any money its first five years in business.[8] Amazon took nine years before recording its first profitable year.[9] While it likely won't take you that long, it can take 18–24 months before turning a profit.[10] The 10X Formula will help insulate you against any setbacks.

YOUR TURN

Write out the **10X FORMULA:**

10X _____ + 10X _____ = 10X _____

Why are both **10X MINDSET** and **10X ACTION** needed to achieve **10X SUCCESS?**

_____
_____
_____
_____
_____
_____
_____

Which tends to be easier for you and why?

_____
_____
_____
_____
_____
_____

THE 10X RULE   11

Take your current goals: # customers, # employees, gross revenue. Now, **10X** them.

Current Goal	10X Goal

What are some of your immediate thoughts that come up when you force yourself to think at a **10X LEVEL?**

_____
_____
_____
_____
_____

10X Goals aren't enough. My goals must be backed by 10X Action.

"Average never inspired anybody."

— GC

CHAPTER 2

AVERAGE IS A FAILING FORMULA

When I was six years old, I sat in a darkened movie theater in Lake Charles, Louisiana, with my father on one side and my grandfather on the other. As I watched the screen in front of me, I saw my future unfold in full technicolor.

The movie: *Goldfinger*. My new idol: James Bond.

I knew, deep in my soul, that I was meant to be a playboy, complete with the bank account, fancy duds, and beautiful women. For the first time in my life, my imagination had been captured, and I was sold.

Even though I don't regularly get in gun fights as I outrun the bad guys, I can make a pretty good case that I've achieved a version of that six-year-old's dream.

What I want to point out, though, is how that vision drove me. After that day, I'd tell anyone who'd listen about my desire to become rich and fly around in private jets. Even though they laughed at me (particularly when I was a loser strung out on drugs), I still had that picture of what it would look and feel like to zip around in an Aston Martin with a Walther PPK within reach and a gorgeous woman by my side.

Notice that I wasn't inspired to become Goldfinger's manservant or any of the guards or even the nuclear physicist. I wasn't inspired by average. I was consumed with the star of the film, James Bond himself.

No surprise, right?

In fact, I bet you've had your own version of my *Goldfinger* experience. Maybe it was wanting to be one of Charlie's Angels or Batman or John Wick or Wonder Woman. These are larger-than-life characters who serve to captivate our imaginations.

But why, then, are we as business owners caught off guard when "average" doesn't inspire our employees, customers, or clients? Why do we expect everyone to want to join us in pursuit of an ordinary goal?

By definition, average means "typical; common; ordinary."[11]

Average never made anyone travel to 100 cities in a month to meet with prospective clients.

Average never made anyone tattoo a logo on their body like Nike or Harley Davidson.

Average never made anyone stay up all night and live at the office in order to meet the launch date.

Average never captured anyone's imagination.

Average never changed anyone's life.

Average is forgotten.

Imagine placing a recruitment ad for new employees:

> *Wanted: Outstanding employee who wants to make an average salary while contributing one-third of your*

waking hours to an average product with average market share. You'll be surrounded by average employees (when they show up) and managed by an average executive team. Must be highly motivated.

See the problem here? You can't scale your business, attract extraordinary team members, create an extraordinary corporate culture, achieve extraordinary growth, earn extraordinary profits, and have an extraordinary impact on the world if you are committed to being only average.

No one wants to pay a premium to eat an average burger, see an average movie, go on an average vacation, or stay in an average hotel. And if they do have an average experience, they're not gonna be bragging about it to their friends and family. We talk about the things that amaze us, wow us, and impress us. "Average" does none of these.

As a leader — and all entrepreneurs are leaders, if you haven't already grasped that concept — you must commit yourself to an extraordinary vision and then share that vision with your team members, customers, and marketplace. You must inspire yourself with an unreasonable mission so they, in turn, can be inspired. This is how you attract employees, customers, and attention. This is how you scale.

If you look at the companies that have no problem recruiting, it's those with unreasonable goals that stand out from the crowd. Tesla, SpaceX, Google, Amazon, Apple ... these companies could fill their recruiting classes many times over without advertising. Why? Because their purpose is so large and captivating that people can't wait to be part of it.

You must do the same. Whether you're a custom T-shirt printer, an insurance agency, or a landscaping business, it is critical to have a vision for your business that not only captures your energy and focus, but also can be shared with others in a vivid enough manner to capture their hearts.

Here's an example: I'm on a mission to reach eight billion people on this planet.

That goal inspires me. Each day, I wake up with that number in front of me. I weigh all my decisions against that benchmark. It keeps me motivated and moving in the right direction, even through the setbacks and hard days.

Impossible? Maybe. But it still serves as my focus, day after day. When I feel tired, discouraged, or distracted by the millions of options in front of me, I come back to this one goal, as out of reach as it may seem.

And largely because of its apparent impossibility and my lunacy, this goal makes people sit up and take notice. It's anything but average, and as a result, by definition it helps me stand out. Some people tell me it's insanity, that I'm an ego-driven maniac. Blah blah blah. But other people open their eyes a little wider and say, "Hey, that's awesome. There's something different about this cat." It's that second group of people who have caught the vision and who I want on my team as employees, audience members, and customers.

No, I probably won't inspire all 8 billion people on earth with my "crazy" goals. But I won't inspire *anyone* with average — and neither will you.

Now you may be wondering how to generate a vision or mission that inspires. Great question. Let's go!

10X MINDSET: IT'S AS EASY TO THINK BIG AS IT IS TO THINK SMALL

One of the biggest misconceptions about setting goals, particularly in regard to growing your business, is that you're better off setting a "realistic" goal. In fact, one of the most popular frameworks for goal setting insists that you set "S.M.A.R.T." goals: specific, measurable, attainable, relevant, and time-bound.[12]

Screw that.

What's attainable for you is completely a matter of belief. The rehab counselor who told me I'd always be an addict, lucky to maintain my sobriety, had one belief about what was "attainable" for my future. I had another. Guess who I chose to listen to? (We'll talk more about dealing with the critics and haters in future chapters, but the main approach to them is to cut them out of your life. They don't matter.)

In fact, I believe that setting what the "experts" would call attainable objectives is the real reason so many business owners don't meet their growth goals.

Why? Because setting your target low almost ensures you will end up at or below it. Starting small means you're aiming small, and it is rare that you will surpass this initial goal. Yes, it can happen — but not very often.

Let's say you own a catering company specializing in weddings and special events. You're doing about five events per month, most of which are in the $5,000 to $10,000 range, and you're generating about $40,000 in revenue each month. It's a nice little business, but you want more.

In your quiet times, you see what you could scale to be: the go-to special events caterer in your region, complete with exclusive contracts with high-end wedding venues, destination wedding catering services, millions of followers on TikTok, your own cookbook series, and a TV show on the Food Network.

But when you share your vision with a few people, they tell you to go slow. "You don't want to grow too fast," they caution. "You could get into trouble that way."

So you lower your goals and think, "Okay, maybe this quarter I'll just aim to get one exclusive contract and increase our average event fee from $7,500 to $8,000. That sounds reasonable."

Because your goals are so "reasonable," you don't have to act on them right away. You increase prices five percent and add a consulting fee to your packages to bump up your average event revenue. And a few weeks before quarter-end, you recall that you were going to try to line up one exclusive deal with a local venue. You make a few calls, and you actually land two of the five you reached out to.

Score! Not only did you meet your goal and increase your average job cost, you landed not one but TWO exclusive deals! You're a rockstar and have blown your goals out of the water!

Rah, rah … but what if you had set your goals higher?

What if you'd said you wanted to land 10 exclusive deals and increase your average job to $75,000? What could you have done if you'd aimed for 10X?

Yes, you'd likely have to hire employees, revamp your entire company, and develop new products and services. You'd likely have some sleepless nights as you deal with vendor issues and financing. You'd probably get in over your head a time or two, but so what? That's what happens when you scale big.

As an entrepreneur, you have gone into business to improve people's lives. To refuse to grow is selfish. If you are a person of integrity, you *must* serve as many people as possible. Imagine having the cure for cancer but sharing it with just a handful of people because you didn't want to "grow too fast." Meanwhile, people are in pain and dying when you could help them!

It truly is as easy to think big as it is to think small. The bigger the goal, the more you will have to shift your mindset … But once you do so, your internal motivation will kick in. You will be forced outside your comfort zone, and in doing so, you will become laser-focused on your new commitment. And from commitment comes creativity. There is no other choice.

And when others see your commitment and excitement, they will get excited, too. You will inspire your employees and customers to join you in this quest.

Will you meet your 10X Goals? I do not know. But I can guarantee that you will achieve more than if you had set small, realistic goals.

Average goals are almost always a letdown to the person setting them (and to their team, customers, and audience). And when you're uninspired, you'll be unable to back your goals with the level of activity necessary to achieve even average results.

10X ACTION: THINK BIG, THEN SHARE THE VISION

You know what the biggest problem you have with your business is? No, it's not supply chain management, hiring, or the competition. It's disengagement: disengagement of customers, of employees, and even of yourself.

The definition of disengagement is "to release or detach oneself, withdraw."[13]

Most of the world is longing to be part of something larger than themselves. Why else do people go nuts when "their" team makes it to the World Series or Super Bowl? It's because they are craving meaning and significance, and they'll take it anywhere they can find it.

That is why it is absolutely essential that once you have set a 10X Goal, you share it with your employees and customers, as well as the larger world, in such a way that they can share in the vision.

According to Gallup, less than 40 percent of your employees are "highly involved in, enthusiastic about and committed to their work and workplace."[14] If only 36 percent of your employees — people you *pay* to be excited about your company — are happy to be there, there is no doubt that the percentage of the general population who care about your business is infinitesimal.

The number one cause of this disengagement is the lack of a life-changing purpose. If your goal isn't going to materially change things, how likely are you to push through the pitfalls and barriers you will inevitably encounter along the way?

Your employees are counting the hours until they can clock out because they are uninterested in or do not share your business's mission.

Your market isn't paying you any attention because they don't even know you exist.

Your current clients are not rushing to tell their friends and family about you because you have not impacted them at a heart level.

You are optional, negligible, and boring.

The way out of this swamp of irrelevance is easy. You must create a 10X vision and take every opportunity to share it with everyone, from the receptionist at the front desk to the guy who empties your trash.

I'm known for my helicopters and private jet with "10X" emblazoned on the tail. Do I livestream from 40,000 feet in order to impress you? Well, I am pretty proud of 'em! But mostly, I do it because I want to share the vision of what my brand means. I want everyone to know what "10X" stands for and to know that you can have it, too. I want you to catch the 10X dream because I know when you do so, you will become a partner, a fan, an employee, a client, or a supporter of some sort. You must do the same for your business.

Once you've determined your 10X Goal, it is now your job to make everyone know about it. It's not just something you put on the wall in your conference room or plaster on the front page of your brochures. It becomes something you live and breathe, and it should inspire others to live and breathe it, too. This is how you create the momentum to scale your business to extraordinary heights.

Love 'em or hate 'em, everyone knows Elon Musk wants to go to Mars, that Walt Disney wanted to create "the happiest place on earth," and that Donald Trump wants to "Make America Great Again." How do we know? Because they told us, over and over. And some of us caught their vision and want to be part of it.

Your 10X Goal must motivate you, and then you must use it to motivate others. When you do so, everything about business growth, from recruiting to customer acquisition, becomes easier.

CHAPTER RECAP

- You can't have an extraordinary impact on the world if you are committed to being only average.
- You must inspire yourself with an unreasonable mission, so others in turn can be inspired.
- Setting attainable objectives is the real reason so many business owners don't meet their growth goals.
- The biggest problem facing you as a business owner is disengagement: disengagement of customers, of employees, and even of yourself.
- Your 10X Goal must motivate you, and then you must use it to motivate others.

GROW OR DIE

**About 75 percent of all businesses in the US have no employees.[15] Only 25 percent of businesses survive more than 15 years.[16] There is no coincidence that these two statistics align almost perfectly.
The choice is simple: Grow or die.**

YOUR TURN

What do you believe about **SCALING** your business that is keeping you **SMALL?**

_____
_____
_____
_____

Write out a **VISION** of your dream for your business that is **AT LEAST 10X LARGER** than your current vision. Does this **MOTIVATE YOU** and get you excited? Will it **MOTIVATE OTHERS?**

_____
_____
_____
_____
_____
_____
_____
_____

10X I refuse to be a statistic! I commit to growth.

> "If you're not afraid, your goals aren't big enough."
>
> – GC

CHAPTER 3

FEAR IS A LIAR

If you want to be successful as an entrepreneur and in life, you must refuse to be ruled by your emotions.

While positive emotions can lure you into a false sense of power and security, I've found that for business owners, it's the negative emotions that you must be particularly vigilant about. Fear, the most damaging of all emotions, can disguise itself as being "realistic," "conservative," or "logical."

Doubt — a nasty byproduct of fear — is the dream killer. Doubt will do more to damage your potential as an entrepreneur than just about anything else. Why? Because your ability to create 10X Goals and follow that commitment up with 10X activity levels depends largely on your belief in yourself and your ability. Once you doubt your abilities, you will cease to take the actions necessary to achieve your goals.

There is a widespread fallacy that somehow successful people never feel fear, and if you do sense uncertainty, anxiety, or downright panic, you are doing something wrong and should retreat until you feel comfortable.

Nothing is further from the truth. Ask any high-level businessperson, and I guarantee they are terrified on a weekly, if not daily, basis.

The difference is that they get used to the discomfort and continue on.

People ask me all the time how I became fearless. I have to laugh because I am one of the most risk-averse people you'll meet. I am regularly scared, but I don't let my emotions determine my actions. You must refuse to do so as well.

Here is just a short list of what has scared me in my life:

- Speaking to an audience of five salespeople when I first launched my sales training business in 1987 when I was 29 years old.
- My first TV interview with Neil Cavuto on Fox News in 2013.
- Interviewing President Donald Trump on stage at GrowthCon in 2022 (I was deathly afraid I was going to say something wrong. Sure enough, my wife gave me a long list of "corrections" after the interview was over!).
- Going skydiving with my wife and jumping out of a perfectly good airplane on purpose.
- Becoming a father.
- Investing in my first serious real estate deal: a $350,000 apartment complex in Vista, California. I had zero money and was scared I'd lose everything.
- Appearing on season two of *Undercover Billionaire* and committing to building a $1 million business in only 90 days, with no resources, contacts, or name recognition, with the whole world watching.

Read over that list and you may relate to some of the items, as you've experienced something similar. Other items may be far beyond your view of what's even possible. And still others may make you wonder why they caused fear in me at all because they're things you do without a thought.

That's the nature of fear. Not only is it personal to each of us, but it's also ever-changing. As long as we continue to act in the face of fear, our comfort zone will continue to expand, and what once caused us to feel like we might pass out now barely registers. Additionally, we begin to view what once seemed beyond the realm of achievable as increasingly possible, even likely.

The takeaway: No matter how accomplished we become, if we are continuing to grow, we will continue to feel fear. That is not optional.

What is optional is how you let that fear impact you. Early on in my career, I decided to let fear motivate rather than discourage me. As I saw others around me become frozen in their discomfort and worry, I chose to live differently.

I believe you have made this same choice. Entrepreneurship is, by definition, risky. And risk (unless you're a sociopath) comes hand-in-hand with fear. You're already used to moving past anxiety and pushing into the unknown. Now you just have to keep going.

I'm not a doctor or scientist, but I have read research that backs up what I have discovered to be true in my own life: The more I move outside my current level of comfort, the greater capacity I have for additional expansion. As you force your brain to create new pathways, you will experience discomfort — sometimes extreme discomfort. But over time, what was once unusual will become commonplace.

Think about hiring your first employee.

If you're like me, that was a huge moment. Suddenly, I was responsible for someone other than myself. Someone else's livelihood depended on me. If I screwed up, it wasn't just affecting me; it was affecting them and their family as well.

Now, decades later, having just one employee on the payroll seems kind of cute. With over 800 employees (and scores more partners, affiliates, and contractors), I wonder why I felt stressed out about having that first team member.

But every time you do something for the first time — pitch investors, enter a new market, launch a product — it's going to stretch you outside your comfort zone. Anxiety, doubt, and fear may be the result of growth. Your job is to persist in the face of those emotions.

Fear is the ultimate bully. It seems insurmountable and all-powerful ... until you kick it in the teeth. Then, and only then, will it disappear, like a bad dream confronting the light of day.

When I feel fear, I focus on my goals. When doubt creeps in, I change my thinking and counter the "what ifs." Your mind can only focus on one thing at a time, and you get to choose whether you're focusing on the fear or on the possibilities.

MOVE FROM FEAR TO FOCUS
TURN DOUBT INTO DRIVE

One tool I use is what I call "feeding the beast" by keeping my attention constantly focused on the future and what I can create.

I think about what will happen as a result of achieving my goals. I think about my family and how I will continue to provide for them. I think about my employees and their families. I think about the housing I will provide for my future tenants. I think about the jobs I'll generate and the result of billions of dollars pumped into the economy. I stoke the fire of my purpose, and that shifts my focus from fear to possibility.

Here's how you can do the same with your goals.

10X MINDSET: FEAR IS NOT BASED ON RATIONAL THOUGHT

As an entrepreneur, you are already used to confronting fear at some level. You have taken a stand for the future. In fact, the definition of the word entrepreneur says as much. The definition of entrepreneur includes risk: "a person who organizes and operates a business or businesses, *taking on greater than normal financial risks* in order to do so."[17] (emphasis added)

Despite your courage, though, how much is fear continuing to impact your daily actions? How often is fear blinding you to potential, simply because something has never been done before or it's outside your comfort zone? For example, you may be afraid to hire or to spend money on ads, or you may be worried about adding necessary systems ... Fear keeps you from expanding.

I see this all the time when working with business owners. They make the initial investment of capital and courage into their business, and then they become preoccupied with protecting what they have. Suddenly, their balls-out approach to life disappears, and they become overly concerned with not taking risks.

They want to stick to the straight and narrow path through the jungle of entrepreneurship, not realizing that there is no path except the one they forge themselves.

They want certainty when the only certainty is uncertainty.

They want fear-free, anxiety-free, worry-free, and risk-free.

That's when you become a "me too" organization, waiting for someone else to step into the unknown rather than assuming the leadership position yourself. When this happens, you have signed the death warrant for your business. You will never dominate and 10X your business when you're operating from a place of worry and fear.

Truth time. There is a possibility that you'll wake up tomorrow, and your business has evaporated. Your financing dries up. A natural disaster (or worldwide shutdown) forces you to close the doors. Your largest client goes bankrupt, owing you a shit-ton of money. A lawsuit is decided against you.

That is the environment in which each and every business owner operates, riddled with risk and uncertainty. It's understandable that you want to pull the covers up over your eyes and protect what you have. But your nice comfy bed isn't where 10X lives.

You can't 10X your business or your life while thinking about guarding your 1X. You can't advance while you're worried about protecting yourself.

Fear is not based on rational thought. It is based on "what ifs" and the bogeyman, and it will steal your growth and your joy if you let it.

Staying small will not protect you from risk. In fact, you are at greater risk when you play small than when you dominate your market (we'll talk more about domination in chapter 4).

You need to constantly ask yourself, "What's the worst that can happen?" For most of us, it involves losing everything and having to start over. If that occurs, so what? This fear is one of the primary reasons I agreed to appear on the second season of *Undercover Billionaire*. I wanted to prove to myself and to the world that it is possible to start from zero (okay, I had a junker truck and $100) and build a successful business worth over $1 million in less than 90 days. I wanted to take the fear of starting over off the table.

The experience did cause me extreme discomfort, and I was afraid that I would fail and tarnish my personal reputation and the 10X brand. It would have been very easy to just say no or to quit partway through filming. But I had something to prove — to myself and to everyone else out there who doesn't have the advantages of birth, wealth, or connections.

To me, starting from zero is not the worst (in fact, I constantly keep myself feeling broke so I keep hustling). The worst that can happen is giving up on myself before I've even seen what I am capable of.

If you're not happy with yourself, you're playing small. If you have more potential, you have to ask yourself what's holding you in place. Most of the time, it's fear. If fear is something you can't avoid, you need to make it work in your favor.

10X ACTION: LET FEAR GUIDE YOU

If fear is holding you back from achieving your potential (and chances are, it is), you must use it as a way to motivate and drive you forward.

One of the best ways I've done this is by using fear as a guide. Here's what happens to the average person. They take some action outside their comfort zone, feel discomfort, anxiety, and fear, and let that fear stop them from further action. It becomes a blazing red, flashing warning sign that says, "Danger! Stop now!"

But every time you give way to fear, it becomes stronger. The imaginary becomes more and more imposing until you can't even think about heading in that direction.

So what's the solution? *Do it anyway.* Use fear, worry, anxiety, whatever you want to call it, as a sign to proceed at rapid speed, with massive amounts of action. When you do so, you will blow past the fear and leave it in the rearview mirror. You must separate emotion from action. How you feel has zero to do with how you perform.

Many entrepreneurs fool themselves into thinking they must have a plan completely figured out before they execute. Unfortunately, not only does the perfect plan not exist, you waste a huge amount of time, money, and effort as you try to compose one.

I have yet to see a business that proceeds exactly as described in its business plan. Instead, a 75-page business plan with carefully designed full-color charts and 10-year projections is usually an exercise in creative writing and fantasy. The only way to know how the market will respond to your product or service is to take it to them and then adjust along the way.

Quit looking for the "right" way to do something. The only "right" way is to act. The only wrong way is to do nothing!

For example, if you are not sure how you are going to convince an investor to partner with you, start talking to investors. You're not going to figure it out from the comfort of your couch with a cold one in your hand.

Wondering if your new advertising campaign is going to work? Get it out there. Same with that blog post or video you're afraid is a little too edgy. Hit the "publish" button, and then record 10 more. There's only one way to find out, and it ain't asking your momma what she thinks.

The only way to figure anything out is to act before you feel ready. That's when you train yourself to take massive action in the face of discomfort.

I am not recommending that you act rashly or without thought. I am telling you that when you're procrastinating because you know what you need to do next but you're putting it off because you're scared, you need to act.

Whatever you fear, you must do it — and you must do it *now*. Ask yourself, what happens if I don't (expand, hire, advertise, spend)? That outcome is what you should be most afraid of.

Let fear guide you, not distract you. Whatever the outcome, you will be able to handle it, and you will be stronger and wiser next time around.

When you act in the face of fear, you convert that fear to power. Fear will always exist. Use it to your advantage.

CHAPTER RECAP

- Doubt and fear are dream killers.
- Successful people get used to the discomfort and continue on.
- Staying small will not protect you from risk.
- Train yourself to take massive action in the face of discomfort.
- When you act in the face of fear, you convert fear to power.

FEEL THE FEAR ... AND DO IT ANYWAY

According to research by *Harvard Business Journal*, virtually all entrepreneurs feel fear, sometimes on a daily basis. The experts' advice: Learn to respond to fear in a positive manner, such as reaching out to a knowledgeable mentor for support or minimizing the effects emotions have on your decision-making.[18]

YOUR TURN

Think of a time when you **ACTED IN THE FACE OF FEAR.** How did it turn out? How did that impact your **CONFIDENCE?**

_____
_____
_____
_____
_____

Pick one thing that you've been avoiding and **do it right now**. **ASK** for the referral. **HIRE** the next employee. **SAY YES** to the speaking opportunity. Jot down some thoughts on how you felt after you **TOOK ACTION.**

_____
_____
_____
_____
_____

10X Convert fear to power.

> "If competition is healthy, then domination is immunity!"
>
> – GC

CHAPTER 4

DOMINATE, DON'T COMPETE

When I hit the ground in Pueblo, Colorado to kick off my *Undercover Billionaire* journey, the task ahead of me seemed impossible. I needed to create a million-dollar business in 90 days, starting with nothing but $100 and questionable transportation. I couldn't use my name, my reputation, my connections, or my money. I even shaved off my hair. Louis Curtis was an unknown, a man without a past and with nothing but his hustle and his word.

The road to that million-dollar valuation was not easy. I got COVID. I faced rejection after rejection. My heart was breaking, spending so much time away from my wife and my girls. But I persevered. I was on a mission to show everyone on the planet that the American dream is not dead and that anyone — not just those blessed with a family name and inherited wealth — can achieve greatness on their terms.

My strategy was exactly what I'm teaching you in this book: 10X Mindset combined with 10X Action. But there was something else I had in my back pocket, a little secret I'll let you in on. I wasn't there to play the game. I was in it to write the rules and create the game. From the first minute I stepped off the plane in Pueblo, my goal was to dominate, not compete.

Everyone loves to compare business to sports, talking about "edging out the competition," "making a team effort," and "leveling the playing field." When people watch sports, though, they usually want to watch a "good game," meaning it's a fair match-up that goes down to the final nail-biting minutes. That's the farthest thing from what you want as an entrepreneur.

As a business owner, you should desire to annihilate others who attempt to enter your market. Amazon, Chick-fil-A, Google, ESPN … these are businesses so far ahead of their "competition" and so dominant that they may as well be a category of one. This kind of "game" may not keep spectators on the edge of their seats until the final buzzer, but it's pretty darned fun for the business owners and shareholders who are raking in the benefits of being the clear leader in their market.

DOMINATION (noun)

1: supremacy or preeminence over another
2: exercise of mastery or ruling power
3: exercise of preponderant, governing, or controlling influence[19]

This is the position I wanted to create for myself in Pueblo, a little western town with higher-than-average unemployment and lower-than-average income. My desire was to create a business that stood alone, causing other business owners in the city to sit up and take notice. My aim was simple: to dominate my category.

That's how Wake Up Pueblo was born (you can find out more about Wake Up Pueblo at WakeUpPueblo.com).

Wake Up Pueblo is a strategic marketing agency that supports local businesses in a way Pueblo had never seen before. With daily content for businesses in every industry from banking to paintball, our goal is to help our clients dominate their markets. We assist them in doing something that I myself have done to take a commanding role in the social media space: massive activity far beyond what most will consider justified, possible, or desirable.

Daily content is something unimaginable for most small businesses. They're happy with a tweet every so often and a monthly email. After all, that's what the *average* company does … And that's exactly why we take our clients in a different direction. Social media is a prime example of what is required to pursue 10X Success: the combination of goals and action to back them up. A video every week is a drop in the ocean of YouTube. If you're creating a tidal wave, you need unstoppable energy and momentum.

When your aim is to dominate, you set the pace. It doesn't matter if other businesses all take three-day weekends and two-hour lunches. It doesn't matter if other businesses wouldn't think of making 100 phone calls in a day. It doesn't matter if other businesses think you're nuts for the level of both your goals and your activity. What matters is that you continue on your own path, playing by your own rules, to win your game, and to be the standard by which all others will be measured.

DON'T COMPETE.
DOMINATE.

When you dominate, your victory is assured. You no longer spend any energy looking at what others are doing because you are the clear leader.

Warning: Others will benefit if you slow down, so they will constantly be telling you to ease up, warning you that you're going to burn out (more on that in chapter 9), and criticizing you for what they call your "insane" efforts. They want to shame you into inactivity because that will allow them to look better and catch up. Don't listen.

I won't give away the whole storyline of my time on *Undercover Billionaire*, but you can imagine how it went. I wasn't going to be content to play by the rules and aim to create a business worth $1 million. I went 10X, baby. I set my goal 10X high and followed it up with 10X Action, with the intent to wake up sleepy Pueblo and dominate the scene. Did I do it? You'll have to watch season two to find out (and when you do, don't laugh at my hair, man).

Quit buying into the lie that competition is the key to success. Domination is where your 10X dreams lie. Here's how to get there …

10X MINDSET: PURSUE DOMINATION

Before you can effectively dominate your market, the first battleground is your mind. You will never be able to truly own your industry and achieve your goals if you are hesitant or afraid of greatness.

You were likely brought up to believe that any competition must be fair, nice people take turns, and you should never run up the score too high on the basketball court or football field. Everyone gets a trophy for "trying hard," no matter who wins, and you end each game with a popsicle and a hug from your mama. It's all about making sure everyone feels good, and no one gets their feelings hurt.

Now I love a hug from Mom as much as the next person, but that's not why I'm in business. And while some have called me a greedy bastard, I'm not in business just to make money, either. My purpose, which drives me day in and day out, is to help others improve their lives, and to create wealth for myself, my family, my employees, and their families along the way.

I'm intent on helping 8 billion people improve their lives through the products and services I sell and the skills I can teach them. This purpose has nothing to do with feelings and everything to do with getting my name out far and wide, whatever it takes — not for my ego, but because I know I can help them.

I was talking to a drywall installer the other day who said he felt guilty about pushing way past the others in his market. "I'm doing good. I have a great life. There's enough business right now for everyone. I don't want to be greedy," Tom told me.

"Look, Tom, bro," I asked him, "are you the best at what you do?"

"Of course!" he answered, his chest puffing out, showing me he was serious. "There's no one who takes as much care as me and my guys do when we're working on a project. We always go above and beyond."

"Then why in the heck would you want any builder or remodeler out there to use anyone else? Do you want them to get below-excellent service?" I asked.

"I never thought about it like that," Tom said.

"If you deliver a superior product or service, you owe it to people to give it to them," I said. "If you are a person of integrity, you are *out of integrity* when you're not helping those who need you."

When we talk about "fair competition," it assumes that all participants have an equally attractive, equally effective solution. I have no problem saying I want to dominate my market because I know that the products and services in all my businesses are far superior to the other options available.

Just like Tom, you are doing a disservice by not serving those you can help. You must have such confidence in the superiority of your business's offerings that you can't sleep at night, knowing there are people out there that you could help but don't yet know your name (we'll talk more about purpose in chapter 9 and how critical it is for you to be in touch with your driving mission).

If you do not feel driven and ethically obligated to get your product into the hands of everyone who can use it, you are never going to be able to effectively establish yourself as the leader in your category. Once you embrace that role, you will be set free. The only thing to do next is to create massive action to support your extraordinary goals.

10X ACTION: SEEK YOUR UNFAIR ADVANTAGE

You may not have been born with the last name "Cuban" or "Trump." You may not have a genius-level IQ or have started coding at age five. If not, don't worry. Me neither.

Maybe you grew up without a dad, like me. Or under severe financial constraints. Or in an environment of violence. Or with physical or mental differences that have made your path harder than most.

Whatever your limitations, you do have something no one else has, something that can benefit you on your journey to domination of your market. It's different for each of us, and it's up to you to figure out what it is and then leverage the hell out of it.

When I went on *Undercover Billionaire*, many of the advantages and strengths I'd developed over my three decades in business were erased the second I emerged in Pueblo as Louis Curtis. My reputation, my bank account, my credit, my name … all gone. But what no one could take away is what I've relied upon since my early days in business: my commitment, my hustle, and my desire to succeed. These became my unfair advantages as I sought to create a million-dollar company. I would continue to pursue my goal, no matter what.

What are your unfair advantages, and how can you unleash them at 10X levels in pursuit of your goals? What can no one else replicate about your experiences, your connections, your assets, or your attributes?

Let's say you're a high-end landscape architect company. You create beautiful, custom outdoor spaces for your high-end clients in the midwest, and you want to massively expand your business. You feel like you've maxed out the market for your current services. What can you do to grow?

Well, as the person who designed the current landscape, you're in a prime position to help your former clients care for their property. You have an unfair advantage in the wealth of information about your client base that puts you in a unique position to suggest other services to them (yard maintenance, winterizing, lighting, painting, pool maintenance, concrete pouring, etc.). You could partner with other companies to provide these services, or you could create a new division of your existing business that handles, say, weekly yard maintenance, which is something that most landscape architects won't touch with a 10-foot pole. You, however, are willing to do what others in your market will not do.

If you want to dominate, look at what others are doing and then do what they won't. Do what they will not do, go where they will not go, and think and take actions to the level they cannot understand or imitate. This is what will separate you from the rest of your market. This is what will allow you to achieve extraordinary success.

CHAPTER RECAP

- As a business owner, you should desire to dominate others who attempt to enter your market.
- When you dominate, your victory is assured.
- You must feel an ethical obligation to get your product into the hands of everyone who can use it.
- Every business owner has something no one else has, something that can benefit you on your journey to domination of your market. Find this unfair advantage and 10X it.
- If you want to dominate, look at what others are doing, and then do what they won't.

AIM FOR OPEN WATER

One of the best ways to *dominate* your market is to *define* your market. These businesses successfully created their own categories and, in doing so, secured a dominant market position where everyone else is a mere imitation of the original:

- *Airbnb* - the first company to offer peer-to-peer lodging
- *Cirque du Soleil* - the original entertainment company that blended acrobatics, theater, and traditional circus acts
- *Kleenex* - the first facial tissue, introduced in 1924
- *Stitch Fix* - the best-known company to offer personal styling services via the Internet
- *Lululemon* - the first company to create high-performance athletic wear and position itself as an aspirational lifestyle brand

YOUR TURN

What would it look like to be the **WINNER IN YOUR SPACE?** What would it look like to **CREATE** your own space?

_____
_____
_____

Double down on your unfair advantage. Maybe you have a **UNIQUE SKILL** (you speak Spanish fluently? Go own a market your competitors can't enter!), or a connection (your aunt writes for the local paper), or years of experience that make you the stand-apart expert in your space. Or maybe, like me, you're committed to doing whatever it takes, however long it takes, to get to your goals. Name your unfair advantages here:

_____
_____
_____

10X When I create the game, I write the rules.

> "If people don't know you for your work ethic, you ain't working."
>
> – GC

CHAPTER 5

OBSESSION IS A GIFT

Hey, I'm Grant, and I'm obsessed.
When I left rehab in my 20s, the alcohol and drug counselor told me I'd never amount to anything because I was defective and was a victim to a disease I had no power over. I was told to focus on my sobriety. "The most successful thing you can do with your life at this point is never use again," my counselor told me in this inspiring "pep talk." "Focus on anything else, and you will fail."

What that counselor did not understand about people like me — and, most likely, about people like you, too — is that, yes, we're obsessed. But we have the ability to decide what we want to be obsessed *about*.

The dictionary defines "obsession" as having your thoughts dominated by one specific goal. It's often used in a negative sense, such as "He's obsessed with his truck," or "She's obsessed with work." But to me, obsession isn't inherently good or bad. It's a tool to be used. And just like you can use a hammer to destroy or to build, your obsession can be directed toward positive or negative outcomes.

WHAT IS OBSESSION?

My definition: Those dreams and goals that you desire to achieve so intensely that they give you the urge, momentum, and energy necessary to build the life you desire and dream of.

Merriam-Webster definition: A persistent disturbing preoccupation with an often unreasonable idea or feeling[20]

In my youth, I was obsessed with the wrong things: drinking, smoking, goofing off. I knew I couldn't change my core personality (that's how I'm wired!), but I could shift the objective of my obsessive nature. Instead of chasing a high or a good time, I would turn my dedication and commitment in a positive direction and become obsessed with success.

From the day I left the treatment center, I locked onto my goal of extraordinary success like a heat-seeking missile. I threw myself into my job as a car salesman. I listened obsessively to tapes on self-improvement and selling techniques. I came in early and left late, and did everything I could to move away from my past. I was channeling all my energy, drive, and time toward a positive goal, and my efforts started to pay off.

From this single decision — to choose a positive target for my obsessive nature — came all future success. Everything, from my businesses to my real estate portfolio to my live events to my relationships, has been the result of my single-minded determination, focus, and unwillingness to stop until I reached my goal. Just as a drug addict is fixated on the next high, I became fixated on staying clean, increasing my skills, and building my business.

GET OBSESSED WITH SUCCESS

Warning: When you go all-in on your goals and devote your creativity, energy, and other resources toward achievement, you will attract criticism and outright hostility.

Start to get in shape, and people will suddenly become "worried" that you're working out too much or not eating enough.

Start devoting more time to your business ideas, and people will suddenly become "worried" that you're working too hard.

Sign up for a marathon, quit drinking, start a new business, or take an online course to finish your degree, and concerned citizens will come out of the woodwork with all sorts of advice, caution, and warnings about what you're doing.

When I made my mindset shift and began directing my energies to work and life success, people around me did not like it, and they were bound and determined to let me know. Early on, coworkers told me that I was working too hard.

When I launched my sales training business, people told me I was on the road too much and I'd burn out.

When I started investing in real estate, people told me I'd hate being a landlord and dealing with high-maintenance tenants.

When I pursued my future wife, Elena, with single-minded determination, calling her every month for a year without her ever answering the phone or even returning my calls, people told me I was acting like a stalker and was going to scare her off.

When I committed to holding the 10X Growth Conference in Marlins Park on Super Bowl weekend in 2019, people told me I would lose my shirt.

When I decided to go on *Undercover Billionaire* and spend 90 days in anonymity, loneliness, and discomfort with the sole goal of building a million-dollar business, people told me it couldn't be done, and I would embarrass myself.

When I announced I was launching 10X Studios, a film and TV production and financing studio, people told me it was impossible and I was wasting my money.

On and on it goes, with an endless line of haters, critics, and "experts" intent on telling me what's wrong with my decisions and how I should live my life. But here's the really interesting thing: The criticism never comes from people doing more than I am; it only comes from those doing less.

That's because your 10X Goals and 10X Action make them nervous. It makes them take a look at their own life and see where they're playing small, settling for average, or just not living up to their own potential.

You must be willing to be an outlier if you are committed to extraordinary success in your business and your life. Get used to "constructive criticism," "loving concern," and feedback from those who would rather spend their time commenting on your behavior than doing something about their own dumpster fire.

Hear me on this: NO ONE achieving at extraordinary levels in their business gets there without obsessive attention to their goals. From the corner deli that has a line out the door at lunchtime to the plumbing service that has nothing but five-star ratings on Google, entrepreneurs who are setting the standard in their markets aren't just concerned with their performance, they're obsessed with it. Not only are they laser-focused on the outcome they desire, they are also relentless in the pursuit. They consistently set 10X Goals and follow them up with what I call Level Four Massive Action.

In the next sections, we'll talk through how to harness both mindset and behavior to support your positive obsessions.

10X MINDSET: CHOOSE YOUR OBSESSIONS

As you build your business, are you getting the criticisms that I've laid out above? Are your friends and family telling you that you're a workaholic, living an unbalanced life, or just plain boring because all you do is work, talk about work, or plan when you're going to work next?

If so, you're in good company.

I've been called ADD, ADHD, OCD, and more. And I've gotten to the point where I see any comments on my obsessive nature to be compliments rather than insults. My obsession is a gift, and it is imperative that you see yours as a gift as well.

Look around at the others in your life. Everyone is obsessed with something. Fantasy football. Sex. Food. Shopping. By now, I hope I've convinced you that being obsessed with your goals is a positive, not a negative.

But how does that obsession play out in your life? And are you using your obsession as a cover for thinking small?

I've seen many entrepreneurs and business owners do just this. They think they're working, and they are, but they're stuck where they are because they're not thinking big enough.

I had an eye-opening encounter with Patricia, who owns a home healthcare agency in Southern California. After several years of steady growth, she was stagnating at about $800K a year in annual revenue and wondering what to do to break the million-dollar mark. "There are so many things to deal with," she told me. "Changing regulations, staffing issues, a shifting demographic profile in our clients, the need for training, liability insurance, and so much more."

"What's your most pressing issue?" I asked her.

"Well, I'm trying to figure out what to do about staffing. That drives revenue, so that's a huge concern."

"What are you *doing* about it?" I asked her.

Patricia looked confused. "The usual. Advertising, offering referral bonuses to current employees. But everyone in the industry is having the same problems. No one can hire these days. I barely sleep at night because I'm wondering how to cover my current client load. I'm never going to hit $1 million if I can't handle the clients I have right now."

Aha! Problem diagnosed.

Patricia wasn't obsessed with success; she was obsessed with her problems. Instead of spending her days driving forward, she was stuck in neutral, wheels spinning.

The difference here is a slight one, so pay attention. It all goes back to mindset. Patricia was focused on $1 million, a goal she believed she should be able to meet with her current levels of activity. What she needed to do was think bigger.

"What does 'success' look like for you?" I asked her. "What do you really want to commit to? What do you want from life?"

She painted a picture for me of making enough money to allow her daughter to come work with her, sending her grandchildren to private school, and maybe establishing a nonprofit to provide mentoring to inner-city kids.

"That's gonna take way more than a million-dollar business," I said. "We're talking 10X. You can do it," I told her. "You just gotta commit to it. That has to be what's keeping you up at night, not where you're gonna hire one more friggin' employee."

When you commit fully, creativity follows. I have no doubt that if Patricia commits to her 10X purpose, she will find a way to bring them to life. Her imagination will be unleashed, and she will be motivated to do what it takes … at 10X activity levels.

10X ACTION: FOUR DEGREES OF ACTION

You've probably guessed by now that being obsessed with success isn't just limited to thinking about your goals; you must back your mindset with 10X Action. But how much action? Answer: MASSIVE action. Here's what that looks like.

I've defined four categories, or degrees, of action:

Level	Description	Result
ONE: Do nothing	No longer taking actions to move yourself forward in order to learn, achieve, or control some area of your life.	Failure
TWO: Retreat	Taking action in reverse, likely in order to avoid pain or other negative outcomes.	Failure
THREE: Take normal levels of action	Taking normal, or average, levels of action.	Average results
FOUR: Take massive action	Taking massive, 10X Action	Extraordinary results

In any area of your life, you will be at one of these levels. It's even likely that you are at different levels in different life areas: Doing nothing with your finances, retreating in your fitness, taking normal levels of action with your parenting, and taking massive action in your business.

Rule of thumb: If you're not where you want to be, it's almost certainly because you are operating at the *wrong degree of action*.

As someone with big goals, you are clear that taking no action or retreating (Levels One and Two) will not deliver. But what people often don't realize is that doing nothing or retreating still requires an outlay of energy. Whether it's through actively avoiding someone or something, justifying your poor performance, or putting up a front that you're totally fine with where you are, you will be expending resources, even at the lowest activity levels.

Average levels of action (Level Three) logically result in average outcomes. What may surprise you, though, is that an average level of action is the most dangerous place to be because it's acceptable. It's within your comfort zone. It's what most people are doing, and therefore, you fit right in with the crowd. But if you want more — if you want to stand out — you must move yourself to Level Four Massive Action so that you can achieve your 10X Goals and create an exceptional life.

Remember our 10X Formula:

THE 10X FORMULA

10X Mindset + 10X Action

10X Success

Extraordinary success calls for extraordinary (massive) action, period. This is what being obsessed looks like: setting your target and being willing to do whatever it takes (including unreasonable choices) to reach what you want.

The distinguishing characteristic of reaching a new level of activity is that you will encounter new problems. Instead of worrying about how she's going to find new employees, Patricia will be thinking about how to upgrade her payroll system to support hundreds of employees instead of a few dozen or how to handle new regulations in the new states she's expanded into. New challenges are better than old ones when they're a sign of growth and success.

Another thing that will happen as you take more action is that people, friends and family alike, will start to grumble and complain. You'll hear more criticism, more feigned concern for your activity level, and more judgments — all because they feel threatened by your success. Get used to it. And get some new friends.

CHAPTER RECAP

- "Obsession" is defined as "those dreams and goals that you desire to achieve so intensely that they give you the urge, the momentum, and energy necessary to build the life you desire and dream of."
- Obsession isn't inherently good or bad. It's a tool to be used as you choose.
- You must be willing to be an outlier if you are committed to extraordinary success in your business and your life.

FOUR DEGREES OF ACTION

- Ø NO ACTION
- ↩ RETREAT
- ✕ NORMAL ACTION
- 10X *MASSIVE* ACTION

- There are four degrees, or levels, of action:
- Only massive action leads to extraordinary success.
- You will know you are on the right track when people start to criticize you and when you create new problems for yourself.

SET YOUR BRAIN FOR SUCCESS

According to the research of Dr. Fred Luskin of Stanford University, we have around 60,000 thoughts per day — and 90 percent of these are repetitive.[21] Why not use this repetition to your benefit? If you're going to think the same thoughts from day to day, make them 10X thoughts!

OBSESSION IS A GIFT

YOUR TURN

Make a list of your **CURRENT OBSESSIONS,** good and bad. Circle the ones that can stay and cross off the ones that **NEED TO GO.** This can include people, addictions, leisure time activities, patterns of thought, etc.

_____
_____
_____
_____
_____

The market favors **THE BOLD** and **THE QUICK** to act. What is one specific way you can take **MASSIVE ACTION** to get your product or service to market faster?

_____
_____
_____
_____
_____

10X **Being obsessed is a full-time job.**

> "I would rather die in expansion than die in contraction. I would rather fail pushing forward than in retreat."

— GC

CHAPTER 6

EXPAND, DON'T CONTRACT

What are you most likely to do when you're faced with the unknown? Many business owners freeze right where they are.

Whether they're dealing with uncertainty about the economy, lack of clarity regarding a financing deal, or simply confusion about the next right business move, the result is the same. They immediately stop all activity, preferring to wait for the road to be clear before moving ahead (Did you correctly identify this as Level One: Doing Nothing?).

Another common response is to retreat (Level Two) — pulling back, eliminating all current spending, and retracting to become as small as possible, almost as if they can simply hide in the sand until the bad times pass by.

Look at how the businesses around you dealt with the economic challenges associated with the economic disruption of 2020–2021. I bet the vast majority responded in one of these two manners. They either rolled over and played dead, locking the front doors and putting up the "Closed" sign, or they retreated by reducing all activities. Their goal was simply to survive until the government told them it was safe and gave them permission to poke their heads outside their doors, like the groundhog Punxsutawney Phil on February 2.

That's not my style, and it's a lesson I learned many years ago. When I wrote the original *10X Rule* in 2011, unemployment numbers and financial instability were out of control, causing many to enter a state of inactivity or contraction.

All around me, business owners in all industries, from services to retail, were turning tail. They were retreating, pulling back as much as possible, cutting staff, advertising, inventory, and more, with the sole goal of making it through the bleak times by becoming as small as they could.

Something in me saw this as an opportunity. As they say, the road to success is never crowded. I could head in the other direction, doing the opposite and taking advantage of others' unwillingness to continue to expand. I cut my own salary as a way to fund expansion in advertising, investments, and key staffing. I exponentially increased my promotional activity, particularly online, because the costs to do so were low. Newsletters, social media posts, email marketing, videos, speaking engagements, webinars — we ramped them all up.

During this time period, I wrote three books and hundreds of articles and blog posts, launched new sales programs, did hundreds of media interviews, and took every chance to continue to get my name out, all while others were cowering like scared little girls. And when the economic tide began to turn, I was so far out in front that it looked like I was the only one in the race. Our reputation, client base, and revenue all grew substantially.

It's been said that insanity is doing the same thing and hoping for a different result. Based on that definition, I don't feel the least bit guilty about saying most of the businesses in America were downright crazy when we were hit with another economic crisis in 2020–2021. Did they learn from what had happened a decade or so earlier? Nope.

Business owners whom I had considered to be bold and courageous gave up at the first sign that the "two weeks to slow the spread" might take quite a bit longer. Look around any town or city in the nation, and you can see shuttered restaurants and empty storefronts, the aftermath of those who chose to simply quit instead of pivot or expand. Over 200,000 small businesses closed permanently due to the pandemic.[22]

You can guess what we were doing: EXPANDING.

There are two groups that do well during an economic downturn.

First are the big guys, the "too big to fail" companies like Amazon, Home Depot, Target, etc. The truth of the matter is that staying small doesn't keep you safe. Being the big guy on the block gives you more insulation against external threats. You usually have more momentum and thus more options.

For instance, Amazon's profit jumped 220 percent during the first year of the pandemic.[23] Yes, more people were shopping online, but Amazon also made strategic decisions to ride the pandemic wave. The company expanded some of its markets and services, and reoriented its inventory toward home staples, home medical supplies, and higher-demand items. It also invested $4 billion into health and safety efforts to ensure its workers could continue to serve customers.[24]

The second group that comes out of a meltdown in a power position includes smaller businesses that decided that this was their do-or-die moment. These business owners chose to do everything they could to grow, despite the current business environment. If they failed? Well, at least they'd go with their boots on. These groups doubled down, made intentional investments, and pivoted to go where the market wasn't.

You've seen these businesses — or maybe you're one of them. It's the fine dining restaurant that created drive-thru options with the same high quality that customers could enjoy at home. It's the studio photographer who launched a campaign for socially distanced "front porch family portraits" and recruited other out-of-work wedding and special events photographers to handle the demand. It's the boutique fitness center owner who hired laid-off personal trainers and began offering outdoor boot camps because the big-box gyms were closed.

EXPAND YOUR MINDSET & YOUR ACTIONS

The time to expand is when everyone else is contracting.

Yes, there are tons of excuses as to why you can't push forward when times are uncertain:

"We can't travel. How are we supposed to reach our market?"

"Everyone's worried about money. They're not going to be interested right now."

"I can't ask my employees to come into work."

"Once things calm down, we can think about growth. Right now, we just need to survive."

But excuses are not the truth. They're justifications that make people feel better about their lack of accountability and results. For every excuse, I'll show you a business owner who faced the same set of circumstances and used it to their advantage. In times of uncertainty, the one who stands up to lead will be the victor.

I made it clear to my team that our approach to the challenges before us was simple: While we could not control what the rest of the world was doing in response to the pandemic, we could control ourselves. In fact, we had a duty and an obligation to do so.

What's more, by controlling our mindset and actions, we could positively impact each other as well as our families, our clients, and our clients' employees and families. While other companies were taking time off, my team was in expansion mode.

This commitment to 10X expansion paid off big. We grew in every conceivable metric, including a 67 percent revenue increase in 2020 that pushed the business over $100,000,000. We added 1 million people to our email subscriber base, added 3.3 million people to our social media followers, grew our team by over 100 people, and more. More importantly, we impacted the lives of tens of millions of people — all because we refused to contract in the face of uncertainty.

Staying small is not a protection strategy. Level Four Massive Action is what will save you.

10X MINDSET: TAKE 100 PERCENT RESPONSIBILITY

As long as you are in business, you will continue to face challenges. Some will be internal to your business. A key employee quits unexpectedly, or your POS system crashes on the busiest day of the year. Other challenges will be external, like a hurricane wiping out your warehouse or the government declaring your business "nonessential."

If you are intent on achieving extraordinary levels of success and constant expansion, you must respond to both categories in the same way. You must assume 100 percent responsibility for everything in your life. You must relinquish the tendency to blame, make excuses, or pass the buck. Everything — good or bad — comes as a result of your actions. It is all caused by you.

I know you're already thinking of 100 things that you didn't cause. The late truck shipment that caused you to miss your deadline and incur a late penalty. The newspaper that misprinted your advertisement, and now you have to honor a lower price that cuts into your margins. The government bureaucrat who refused to approve your permit. How can you continue to expand with all these idiots in your way?

I would argue that by adopting the mindset that these things happened because of you (not to you), you will exponentially increase your creativity and your ability to find a solution to the challenges you face. You will also decrease the likelihood that the same situation will occur in the future.

"Whoa there, Grant!" you may be saying. "I didn't cause the supply chain issues. We gave the cranky customer perfect service. And no one can control a government bureaucrat! How in the heck am I responsible?"

Well, since you asked …

You could have double-checked to ensure that the shipment was going to arrive on time, and when it was clear it was going to be delayed, you could have forewarned your client. Or you could have built buffer time into your schedule or negotiated the late fee.

For the newspaper, you could have double-checked the ad copy before the paper went to print or supplied your own print-ready art.

And yes, government bureaucrats can be temperamental, but you could have met with them prior to submitting your permit application to ensure everything was approved and ready to go.

In any of these situations, playing the victim does nothing to help you continue to expand. Yes, it can feel good to have someone to blame for our shortcomings, but blame is nothing more than a strategy for failure. No one who has reached extraordinary success in their field has done so by blaming others. And as someone aiming for 10X business and personal goals, you must assume responsibility for everything.

Blaming others puts you in a victim mindset which is by its very nature a position of contraction. Once you make that mental shift to ownership, you will see more options and opportunities open up for you, and more expansive thinking will follow. That mindset is required to equip you to take the actions required to achieve your 10X Goals.

10X ACTION: GO IN THE OPPOSITE DIRECTION OF THE MARKET

Do what everyone else is doing, and you'll get what everyone else is getting.

In other words, take average (normal) actions and get average (normal) results.

There is something comforting about staying with the crowd. It's hardwired into us to want to be one of the pack. Probably because, back in the caveman days, it decreased the likelihood we'd be eaten by the wooly mammoth.

It can be very uncomfortable to separate yourself from everyone else and proceed on your own. You risk ridicule and failure, things most sane people try to avoid at all costs. But as an entrepreneur, you've already committed to being different and standing out. Remember the definition of an entrepreneur: one who takes on greater than normal risks.

Though it may feel uncomfortable, expanding in times when others are cutting back and retreating will secure your position more than any other single activity. Just be prepared for the response from others. They won't like it when you break rank and start doing something different, particularly when your efforts bring results!

I saw this firsthand in the Global Financial Crisis of 2007–2008 that caused an upheaval in the financial and housing markets. Despite what everyone else was choosing to focus on, I was intent on expansion. It was during this time that I wrote *Sell to Survive*, which became a bestselling book and later a part of Cardone University. My goal was to help the huge number of employees displaced from long-standing industries that had seemed indestructible. Not everyone liked my actions, and I was attacked and criticized.

During the pandemic, the same situation occurred. Many states enacted stay-at-home orders that required all businesses to close their doors unless they were deemed "essential" by the government. Most businesses obeyed, at great cost. But a handful refused to close their doors. From a hairdresser in Oregon to a restaurant in Southern California to a gym in New Jersey, business owners with balls said, "No. I'm not shutting down. I am not a victim. You have no right to take my livelihood from me while strip joints and liquor stores are allowed to remain open."

The backlash was immediate. Death threats, boycotts, personal attacks, and more plagued brave people who dared to go against what they considered arbitrary mandates. They continued to cut hair, serve meals, and train gym-goers. They welcomed new customers who had been turned away by other businesses that had chosen to comply — and they got a heap of free press, too.

I won't weigh in on their decisions other than to applaud their courage for continuing to do what they believed was right in the face of great opposition.

The results of their willingness to stand against what others were doing and to forge ahead have been mixed. Some businesses thrived, and some closed down. Some business owners are still doing what they were before, and some pivoted and are involved in something completely different. But none of them has to wonder what would have happened if they'd just kept moving forward when everyone else was in retreat. That's my idea of success.

CHAPTER RECAP

- Many business owners freeze or retreat when faced with uncertainty.
- The time to expand is when everyone else is contracting.
- By controlling our mindset and actions, we can have a positive ripple effect on the world around us.
- If you are intent on achieving extraordinary levels of success and constant expansion, you must assume 100 percent responsibility for everything in your life.
- You cannot contract your way to your goals.
- Expanding in times when others are cutting back and retreating will secure your position more than any other single activity.

BORN TO THRIVE

Being born in hard times just might make you more resilient. These ten companies were all founded during economic recessions:[25]

1. Hewlett-Packard
2. Hyatt Hotels
3. Microsoft
4. Electronic Arts
5. Mailchimp
6. Uber
7. Airbnb
8. Slack
9. Warby Parker
10. Venmo

YOUR TURN

In what areas are others in your market (or in your office) **RETREATING** or **CONTRACTING**? What does expansion look like in these situations?

_____
_____
_____
_____

What's one **SPECIFIC ACTION** you can take right now that makes a **STAND FOR EXPANSION?** Can you get on a new social media platform, send out handwritten thank you notes, or take an afternoon and film 100 short videos? List it here, then put it on your calendar.

_____
_____
_____
_____
_____

10X — The best time to expand is when others are contracting.

> "Resources are only limited to the extent you limit your imagination and action."
>
> – GC

CHAPTER 7

LEVERAGING YOUR RESOURCES

One of the biggest mistakes in my business career was staying small for far too long. Other than for Danny Devito and Kevin Hart, small doesn't work. Small departments, small divisions, small products, small prices — none of it works, man. It took me a while to learn this.

When I first started my sales training business in my late 20s, I prided myself on going solo. I didn't need a team. That meant overhead, and I had been trained from an early age that to make money, you had to keep expenses low. If I hired anyone, that was money coming out of my pocket.

But that meant I was on the road upwards of 275 days a year, traveling constantly and trying to do everything myself. Booking appointments?

That was me. Giving sales presentations? Me. Following up with customers? Me. Billing? Me. Accounts payable? Me. Developing new course materials, printing, order fulfillment? All me, me, me.

After a long day of making sales calls or conducting training sessions, I'd head back to my hotel room and make phone calls, follow up on orders, book my next appointments, and try to keep it all moving forward until I got a few hours of sleep and got up to do it again. There was no such thing as a weekend or a day off. If offices weren't open for an American holiday like Labor Day, I'd head up to Canada and make calls there.

As you know by now, I have no problem with hard work. In fact, I consider it my ethical duty to hustle. But I wasn't just working hard, I was working stupid and hard, and that's a loser's recipe.

I did the same thing with my other resources. I was always watching the clock, worried about "saving time." I also refused to spend money even when it was warranted. I was treating my business like a cheap date, and it was responding likewise.

I had big dreams — that wasn't the problem. I had set my sights on creating a massive training company, one to rival the "big guys" whose videos and tapes I'd studied so religiously. But I wasn't setting myself up for greatness. My refusal to invest my resources and my commitment to doing it all myself while pinching every penny until it squealed were keeping me small.

I was cheap. I didn't spend money because I thought I was supposed to save money. I thought I was doing the right thing. I was following what I'd been trained to do by other business owners: Cut costs, keep overhead low, do it all yourself, and stay lean and mean. Money doesn't grow on trees. A penny saved is a penny earned, and on and on and on. I was brought up to do everything on the cheap. Buy low, sell high.

But here's the problem. That well-intentioned advice I'd been raised on was all wrong. It was average advice for those who wanted to live an average life, and that wasn't me. We have already determined in this book that average doesn't work in any area of life. Anything that you give only average amounts of attention to will start to subside and will eventually cease to exist. I didn't know it, but things would have to shift dramatically in order to create the level of business success I wanted.

Even as my company grew, I begrudged every time I had to spend money or hire someone. I treated it as money out of my pocket, like someone was taking something from me. I kept hold of tasks and responsibilities that were far outside my zone of genius, just so I could avoid increasing headcount.

It wasn't until I started thinking of my employees' salaries as investments rather than expenses that I was able to experience massive growth.

I've seen many business owners make this shift in perspective. They want to hire the top people, but they don't want to pay them top wages. It's ridiculous to think about getting cream-of-the-crop players when you're offering bottom-of-the-barrel prices. Once I understood that my people were assets who could create a positive ROI, I couldn't hire fast enough. People do not cost money. Even bad people don't cost money. Not making money costs money.

Let's say I meet a real superstar, someone who gets the whole 10X concept. They're motivated, high-performing, have a track record of success, and would be a valuable addition to my team. Why on earth would I try to lowball them, offering them slightly less than the industry average? I'm gonna give them *more* than they can get anywhere else for two reasons. I don't want them working for anyone else, and I want them to be happy to come to work every day. I want them to feel like I take such good care of them that they'll go to the moon and back for our company.

Right now, we're experiencing a shift in the way people view employment. No longer do people stay with the same company for their entire career, retiring after decades of loyal service. Instead, our workforce is incredibly volatile. According to one study, the average amount of time people in the 25 to 34 age range stay at a job is just 2.8 years.[26] Combine this with the fact that over 75 percent of workers feel that they're underpaid in their current job,[27] and you can see the problem.

Once you start paying people better, you'll get — and keep — better people.

I've found the same principle to be true in other areas of resources as well. I no longer seek to "save time," which is a physical impossibility. Instead, I want to multiply time. I do this by investing in the people, tools, and technologies that will allow me to work more effectively. I invest my money in assets that will help grow my business or those that will allow me to reduce my expenses.

For instance, you won't catch me wearing a $500 Gucci baseball cap. That, to me, is a waste of money. What you will see me wearing, though, is a branded 10X cap. Not only does it look amazing on this handsome mug of mine, it is also an investment in my brand — and it's tax-deductible. I've turned what could be an expense into an asset.

As a business owner, your success depends on your ability to grow your vision. And that starts with adopting a mindset of leveraging your assets.

10X MINDSET: USE IT OR LOSE IT

If you are going to create massive success in your life and your business, you must believe that your resources are renewable and will replenish the more you use them. Rather than thinking every dollar, every minute, every idea has to be squirreled away for fear another one won't be available in the future, you must adopt a perspective of abundance. If you are operating from a place of scarcity, you will never grow your business to extraordinary levels.

From your energy to your creativity to your money, you have to move away from a "saving" mindset. Just as you cannot save today's hours and bank them to use next week or next year, your energy, money, and other resources are meant to be used now. Money is useless until it's used. The same thing with time, energy, and ideas. They mean nothing until you do something with them.

LEVERAGE RESOURCES TO MULTIPLY THEM

When I hear of business owners underinvesting in their business and then wondering why they're not growing, it makes me nuts. Here's an example. I was at one of our 10X Business Boot Camps a couple of years ago. One gentleman told me about a problem he was having with his real estate investment club. "Everything's on me," Sunil told me. "If I'm doing it, things are happening. If I'm not there, it stops because I'm the one providing the motivation and direction."

We went through the numbers, and the problem was clear. "Your business is broken," I told him. Even though he was generating several millions of dollars per year in top-line revenue, the numbers were too small. Once taxes and expenses were taken out, there wasn't enough there for him — or for any partners he wanted to bring on. "Don't look at how to go from $2 million to $2.2 million," I told him. Looking for incremental changes and investing to make that happen won't get the answers Sunil needs. Instead, he needs to take on the 10X Mindset and figure out how to get to $20 million, using everything he has right now to make that happen.

When you're trying to figure out how to just get up the steps, you don't initially think, "Hey, we should just build an elevator." But why not? Sure, an elevator costs more, but it will save time and make you more in the long run.

Common wisdom is that you have to crawl before you can walk and walk before you can run. Everyone forgets you can just jump. If Sunil doesn't jump and start thinking about a $20 million business, he will cease to exist. You have to get big, period.

Sidenote: Accountants may be the worst possible people to get advice from (no offense to the many great accountants out there!). If you talk to your accountant, they're going to try to convince you to manage money. *But managing money is not an entrepreneurial activity. Their job is to AVOID risk and CONSERVE assets ... which is the opposite of what we often need to do as entrepreneurs. As an entrepreneur, your job is to take on greater than normal risk in order to create more — more value, more money, more success. That requires a shift in your mindset and* your actions.

10X ACTION: MULTIPLY YOUR ASSETS

Just as you can't contract your way to safety (as we discussed in chapter 6), you can't save your way bigger. You can never save enough money to become profitable and experience massive growth. At some point, you have to make money and invest in people, processes, and infrastructure. You have to scale.

Stop thinking about saving money. I'm not interested in saving money. I'm interested in using money to have more money. I don't want to sit here with money in my pocket. I want my money working for me. Rich people invest money. Letting your money sit unused in a bank is another lie poor people believe. Even with compound interest, the current interest rates don't even outpace inflation. Every day your money sits in a bank is a day you're waking up with less than you had the day before.

Money in the bank is stupid. The only one who wins when you have money in the bank is the bank! Cash is not king. Cash is trash. Instead, find ways to put that money to work for you in your business.

When I was on *Undercover Billionaire,* one of the first deals I struck was with business owner Matt Smith. He agreed to give me $6,000 to use to promote his mattress store. Yeah, sure, I could have taken some of that money and spent it on creature comforts, a better place to live, a fancy dinner ... or saved it for a rainy day, which is what I hear a lot of people doing. Instead, I worked for free. I poured every penny into promotions — signage, printing, ads — to make the one-day, blowout sale a huge success. I knew if I could show him a successful campaign that $6,000 would be a drop in the bucket compared to what we'd do together in the future. It was an investment, and it paid off (and it got me a snazzy pair of blue satin pajamas!).

We are programmed to conserve time, energy, and money. But you should look for every opportunity to expend all of the above. The way to get more energy is to use the energy. The way to get more money is to use the money. The way to get more time is to use the time you have. People ask me all the time how I get so much done. I do stuff, dude! The more I do, the more I get done.

At its core, money is just energy. Expend energy to get energy. Expend money to get money. Take massive action, and you will be rewarded. Not every investment you make will pay off, but when you're operating at an extremely high level of activity, the law of averages will work in your favor.

CHAPTER RECAP

- You cannot simultaneously grow your business and stay small.
- Once you start paying people better, you'll get — and keep — better people.
- As a business owner, your success depends on your ability to grow your vision.
- You must believe that your resources are renewable and will replenish the more you use them.
- Look for every opportunity to expend time, energy, and money.

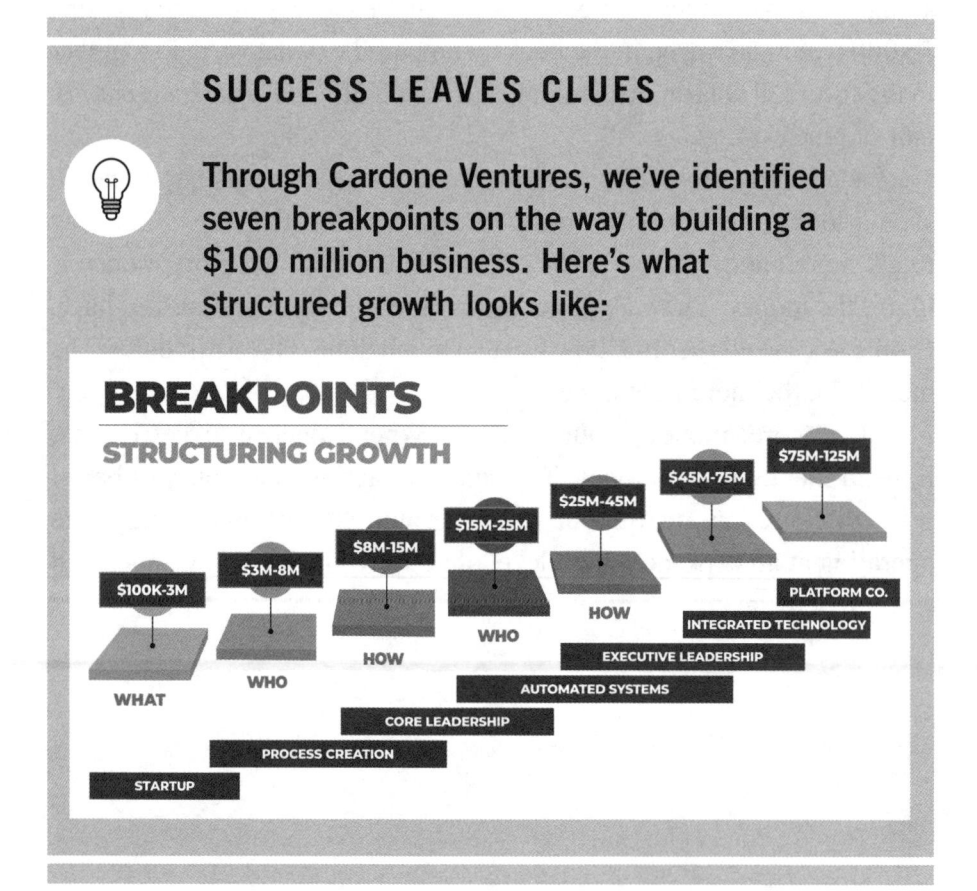

SUCCESS LEAVES CLUES

Through Cardone Ventures, we've identified seven breakpoints on the way to building a $100 million business. Here's what structured growth looks like:

BREAKPOINTS
STRUCTURING GROWTH

Stage	Range	Focus
STARTUP	$100K-3M	WHAT
PROCESS CREATION	$3M-8M	WHO
CORE LEADERSHIP	$8M-15M	HOW
AUTOMATED SYSTEMS	$15M-25M	WHO
EXECUTIVE LEADERSHIP	$25M-45M	HOW
INTEGRATED TECHNOLOGY	$45M-75M	
PLATFORM CO.	$75M-125M	

LEVERAGING YOUR RESOURCES 79

YOUR TURN

Most of us have a tendency to hold tight to **SCARCE RESOURCES**. In what areas of your business have you become a **HOARDER?** (Time, money, ideas, energy, etc.)

_____
_____
_____
_____
_____

What's one way you've been **REFUSING TO SPEND MONEY** (or another scarce resource), and it's **HOLDING YOU BACK?** What are you going to do to **OVERCOME THAT HESITATION?**

_____
_____
_____
_____
_____

10X

I have to scale to be great.

"Love me or hate me, at least you know me."

— GC

CHAPTER 8

OMNIPRESENCE

When I talk about the need to have people know who you are, I often bring up my time on *Undercover Billionaire*. No other experience in my life has so fully driven home the need for businesses and entrepreneurs to have name recognition. Not until I was a complete stranger ("Louis Curtis") in a strange land (Pueblo, Colorado) did I realize how much my reputation and my brand meant to me.

When you are in business, it's better to be hated than to be unknown.

Think about going to the store and looking for laundry detergent. Not only do you have to choose if you want powder or liquid or a pod or tablet, you also have to select from among dozens of brands. So what does the average person usually do? They reach for the brand they recognize. Is it the best laundry detergent out there? Who knows … but it's the one they feel most comfortable with. After all, if everyone is talking about Tide, it can't be that bad. It's the safe bet.

The same goes for your business. Whether you're a fitness center or tire shop or accountant or dry cleaner, having name recognition in your market gives you a huge advantage. It opens doors; it smoothes roads; it engenders trust in people who don't even know you but who have heard of you. Just like the laundry detergent, how bad can you be if they know who you are? When you have name recognition, people will give you the benefit of the doubt.

That's why life was so difficult in Pueblo. I'd lost all my name recognition. All the goodwill and awareness I'd built up over three decades of business was gone. As Grant Cardone, people might not be sold on me, or even like me, but they'll take a meeting with me, even if it's just to see if I'm as crazy as people say I am. But as Louis Curtis? I was a big zero. Actually, worse than zero because I didn't even have entertainment value.

I was still the same person with all the same skills and knowledge and experience — but no one knew it. No one in Pueblo, Colorado, had ever heard of Louis Curtis — and neither had I! He had an empty resume, no relationships, no street cred, and absolutely no visibility in a market in which I had to create a million-dollar business in 90 days.

My problem wasn't lack of knowledge or skills — my problem was irrelevance and obscurity. No one knew who I was or what I could do for them. That's why my first job was to make myself known.

That's why, as an entrepreneur, your primary aim is to raise the level of recognition around you and your business. Getting financing, doing deals, hiring employees, negotiating contracts … it's all much more difficult when no one knows who you are.

Your first and most important goal as a business owner is omnipresence.

The word "omnipresence" is a compound of two parts: "Omni," meaning "in all ways or places," and "presence," meaning "the state or fact of existing, occurring, or being present in a place or thing." Put them together, and "omnipresence" refers to the concept of being everywhere, in all places, at all times.

OMNIPRESENCE (noun)

OMNI (in all places/everywhere)

PRESENCE (being present)

In my mind, there is no such thing as "too well known" or "overexposed." Think I'm wrong? Consider the things in our world that everyone depends upon. Good Wi-Fi. Clean water. Air. Would you ever say, "Darn, that oxygen is way overexposed. There should be less O_2 in the world." No way, José. No matter how much air we have, we still value it. That's why your goal is to be everywhere.

My goal is to reach eight billion people in the world. It's not because I want to feed my ego. It's not because I need more money. It's for one very simple reason: I am 100 percent all-in and fully committed to helping everyone on the planet create unreasonable amounts of wealth, freedom, and success. To help people and to improve their lives, they have to know about me.

What about you? If you are fully sold on your 10X dreams and you are committed to helping as many people as possible, then you cannot be satisfied with being an average fish in an average pond. You need to be a damn WHALE, my friend, the creature in the ocean that everyone is watching out for, that all other sea life is aware of at all times. You must pursue omnipresence because omnipresence brings opportunity. Whatever makes up your definition of success, it's all much, much easier when everyone knows your name.

You've likely experienced this, especially if you're entering a new market or early in your days as a business owner. It's much harder to create momentum from zero. The "big dogs" like Amazon, Nike, Apple, and Coca-Cola ... they spend billions on advertising, so when you go into a store, you grab their products without even thinking about it. We look for and choose what's familiar, even if there might be a "better" alternative.

How else do you explain the existence of McDonald's in Italy? Here you are in the country with arguably the best food in the world. I've never had a bad meal in Italy. Even the hole-in-the-wall bistros are amazing. Yet there's still a line for a Big Mac. Why? Because people recognize the name. They opt for the familiar.

Get known or go broke. It's that simple.

Don't have the cash to throw down for a Super Bowl ad or a full page in *Wired*? You're still not off the hook. Make up for your lack of money with commitment, creativity, and hustle. Here's how to get started with a shift in mindset.

10X MINDSET: SATURATION, NOT SATISFACTION

"Grant, I don't understand what you mean about customer satisfaction," Renata told me at a recent event. A health consultant, Renata had picked up on one of my comments, and it had her stuck. "You say customer satisfaction is the wrong target. Don't we want our clients and customers to be happy?" she asked.

Here's what I told Renata and what I'll tell you: I'm not interested in making people happy. I'm interested in having people buy my product. I'm not going to take responsibility for the emotional state of everyone who reads this book, takes a training course, or watches one of my YouTube videos. That's not my job.

My job — and your job as an entrepreneur — is to create a solution to a client's or customer's problem and then get that solution into the hands of as many people as possible.

This is where many business owners make a huge mistake by focusing on customer service as their end goal. Of course, you want those who buy your product to be happy, but there are two main problems with this line of thinking. First, you cannot help anyone if they do not know who you are. Awareness precedes a buying decision, always. You could have the cure for cancer, and if no one knows about it, you are helping no one.

Second, you are not responsible for anyone else's happiness. There are people out there that you will be unable to please because they're unhappy people. Is that on you? No. They wouldn't be happy if Beyoncé and Jay-Z themselves hand-delivered their purchase to their door and put on a free concert on their front lawn. "I don't like hip hop." "The music's too loud." "What is she even wearing?" You get the picture.

This is what I was trying to relate to Renata, the health consultant. It's far better to serve many people, knowing some will always be less than perfectly satisfied, than to hold onto your product in the hopes of "perfecting" it.

A better mousetrap, lower prices, better service, a better product ... none of it matters if you live and operate in obscurity. An inferior product that is well known can have more impact than a superior product that is unknown.

Think again about the biggest brands in the world. You can find shoes that are more comfortable than Nike — but we still buy Air Jordans. You can find a cup of brew that is objectively better than a Starbucks coffee — but we still buy Starbucks. I know many people who say Google's search engine sucks — but they still use it. Why? It's easier to default to the best-known option, and because of the vast amounts of money these companies spend on branding, everyone knows who they are. Their omnipresence in media, on the sides of buildings, on billboards, on television, and in movies and other media ensures that when you think "sports shoes" or "coffee" or "search engine," you think "Nike," "Starbucks," and "Google." And the more you use them, the more you're likely to use them in the future.

You can do the same thing in your business and cement your role as the industry default. Commit to omnipresence, and choose to raise your awareness to extraordinary levels.

Unless people know who you are, no one will pay attention to what you are creating.

If no one pays attention to what you're creating, they will not purchase.

If they do not purchase from you and become a customer, you are unable to create an impact.

It works in reverse as well. The more attention you get, the greater the impact you and your company can make. The first step? Mindset. The second? Massive Action.

10X ACTION: BE OMNIPRESENT

Your decision to raise your name and brand recognition will mean nothing without Massive Action (Level Four). You must follow up your mindset shift with 10X Actions and do so consistently — even if you are bootstrapping your business and have limited promotional dollars.

One of the most memorable scenes from *Undercover Billionaire* is the sight of me, wearing navy blue satin PJs and a sleep mask, standing by the side of the road and waving customers into the parking lot of Matt Smith's mattress store. The problem Matt and many businesses face is that their businesses appear unremarkable, unnoticed, and irrelevant. To get customers, I had to first get on their radar. That involved signage, balloons, and (you got it) the satin pajamas. And it worked. The sales from that day far outpaced any other single-day sales.

Did we improve our products or customer service? Nope. All we did was raise the public's awareness of the store, make them think about buying a new bed, and get them in the door. Once they were in the store, we could sell to them. The process must work in this order. A purchase cannot take place unless awareness and attention precede.

Your efforts cannot cease with a one-day sale or weekend promotion. To take your business to 10X levels, you must become active in communities where your customers (and your future employees) are, online and off. You cannot be too well known or too familiar. Brainstorm where you need to be, and show up — again and again and again. Give interviews, host a podcast, and court the local newspaper and TV reporters. Let them know you're always available for perspective on topics associated with your business. Suggest story ideas — not just once but weekly.

In this day and age, there is absolutely no excuse for not having a social media footprint. You don't have to be on all platforms, but choose a couple and dominate. One video a week on YouTube is nothing — upload them daily. One tweet a day is irrelevant. Tweet hourly, if not more. Provide value, share tips, and promote your clients and customers. The content ideas are endless once you stop worrying about getting it right and start worrying about just doing it — to massive levels, of course.

Show up to the point that people say, "I see you *everywhere!*"

Remember, you are not in the insurance business, the tech business, the accounting business, or the coaching business. You are in the people business. Focus on meeting and serving as many people as possible, expanding what I call your "power base," those people who already know, like, and trust you. The more people you know — and who know you — the larger your power base. When you focus on expanding your power base through meeting and serving more people, your power base grows. Then your business growth will follow.

CHAPTER RECAP

- When you are in business, it's better to be hated than to be unknown.
- Get known or go broke.
- Your job as an entrepreneur is to create a solution to a client's or customer's problem and then get that solution into the hands of as many people as possible.
- The more attention you get, the greater the impact you and your company can make.
- Show up to the point that people say, "I see you *everywhere!*"

GO WHERE YOUR CUSTOMERS ARE[28]

Aiming for ...	Go to ...
College graduates	LinkedIn (50% of college graduates use it)
Female shoppers	Pinterest (70% of users are female, and more than 75% use it to find new products)
Teens	TikTok (41% of users are in the 16–24 age group)

YOUR TURN

What are some **SPECIFIC WAYS** you can increase **YOUR VISIBILITY?** List 10 (or 100!). Put a star next to three you can do in the next **24 HOURS.**

_____
_____
_____
_____
_____
_____
_____
_____
_____
_____

EXECUTE on the **THREE ITEMS** you starred.

10X

To change the world, the world has to know my name.

> "Burnout is an indication that you are now clearly off your purpose."
>
> – GC

CHAPTER 9

BURN IT DOWN OR BURN OUT

Entrepreneurial burnout is such a concern that experts at leading business schools like Harvard, Stanford, and Wharton are constantly researching and writing about it.

I guess it's a good thing I didn't go to business school!

I don't buy into the whole "working too hard leads to burnout" BS. (No coincidence that "business school" is abbreviated to BS, right?)

In fact, despite being told for most of my life that I'm working too hard and am going to burn out, the only time I've lost momentum and energy is when I've lost sight of my purpose. If I forget why I'm taking Level Four Massive Action, then the door opens for doubt and negativity.

When I'm on mission, hustling for a purpose and in support of my dreams, I'm in the zone. Just like a baseball player rounding third and trying to beat the throw home, I'm not thinking about the ache in my legs, the burn in my chest, or when I last had a day off. I'm laser-focused on the goal — sliding into home base before the throw from centerfield finds its mark in the catcher's mitt. There is no time for doubt or questions. Everything else disappears.

Some might call that obsessed, as we discussed in chapter 5. But as any athlete (or successful entrepreneur) can tell you, there is no success without that intense, all-encompassing focus.

Lose your focus, and you will lose your edge. And what causes you to lose your focus? Losing sight of your purpose.

STAY FOCUSED ON YOUR PURPOSE

I found this out firsthand in my late thirties when I was running my sales seminar business. When I wasn't on the road, I was handling the back end of my business or working on my consulting business. I often lost track of what day it was because it didn't matter. Saturday or Wednesday, I was working, period.

This went on for several years without issue, but then I started to feel off. Lower energy, general irritability, a slowing of my usually unstoppable drive … my passion was flagging, and I began to dread getting back on a plane when it felt like I'd just gotten home.

If I felt these symptoms today, I'd know exactly what the problem was. But back then, I was young and stupid and started wondering if all those critics in my life had been right — I'd worked myself too hard for too long and was starting to feel the results of extended effort. I took some time off, took a look at my diet and made some adjustments, and even started meditating. If I was burning out because of my drive and ambition, the solution had to be to slow down, right?

Wrong. In fact, slowing down made the problem worse. The less I worked, the less I wanted to go back to work. Apparently, "taking it easy" wasn't the answer.

So I dove into fact-finding mode. I sat down and took a life inventory. I had been unstoppable when I'd launched my businesses. Something had happened, but I didn't know what. If it wasn't my health or fitness level, what was it?

I sat down with a piece of paper and started with a full inventory of my life. When had I lost my energy? What had changed? When had my energy started to crater? What made it worse? Did anything make it better?

The answer came to me in one big kick upside the head.

My exhaustion had nothing to do with my physical state at all. It was *mental*.

If we take another look at the 10X Success Formula, two elements are needed: one mental and one action-oriented. I had lost my edge because I'd lost my purpose. I was missing the 10X Mindset.

THE 10X FORMULA

10X Mindset + 10X Action

10X Success

My original goals as an entrepreneur — to launch my sales training business, to give X number of presentations per month, to make an additional Y amount of dollars with my consulting — were no longer feeding me. I wasn't inspired by them. They were dull and boring and way too small for where I now was — and way too small to motivate me to get on yet another plane or work yet another 16-hour day. I'd been chasing the carrot and grabbed it, and my body said, "Okay, why are we still running?"

Once I diagnosed the issue, the solution was easy. I needed to regain my 10X Mindset by defining new 10X Goals that required my obsession. I needed to stretch beyond my comfort zone. Just like that runner who is obsessed with making it to home plate, I needed business and life goals to force me to think creatively and to take Level Four Massive Action.

I allowed myself to dream big and then challenged myself to dream even bigger. I stopped thinking about a solo business and embraced growth. I committed to huge 10X Goals and immediately felt the energy and creativity start to fuel me again.

Entrepreneurs are not meant to live a life of ease. We are meant to set the freaking world on fire. It's in our DNA, and if we deny that by trying to "take it easy," we are going against our very nature. If we don't feel challenged by our work, we will be left depressed and uninspired.

This is what many people don't understand about mega-successful business owners. They don't keep working for the money; they are working because it's what keeps them alive. People like Elon Musk, Bethanny Frankel, and Jeff Bezos (and you and me) can't not work. It's a punishment to take away our ability to grow.

Stop fighting this. It's not a personality flaw or a defect. It's a gift. Whatever you're pursuing, you must go after it with full intention and full energy. In other words, you must be obsessed with your purpose. Rather than sapping your energy and drive, the pursuit of your 10X Success will call forth the best in you as it pushes you to new levels of thinking and new levels of activity.

10X MINDSET: COMMIT TO YOUR PURPOSE

One thing many business books fail to disclose is the idea that your personal purpose as an entrepreneur will evolve as you evolve. The business growth path, while not always linear, is typically predictable.

Growth involves new markets, new customers, new products and services, a bigger presence, and more revenue.

But as an individual, your purpose on day one of your business can be substantially different than what motivates you when you've been in business for five years, ten years, or more. In the early days, you might want to simply see if you have a viable business idea. Once you've reached that milestone, you then might want to create a lifestyle, gain financial security for your family, impact more people, or start a nonprofit. The sky's the limit when it comes to defining your 10X Success.

While I don't know what your personal purpose is, I do know this: If you don't allow your purpose to evolve, if you don't have a purpose with which you are obsessed, if you don't know why you're spending untold time and other resources building your business, you're going to have trouble staying motivated. To have an extraordinary life, you must continuously push yourself to your edge, testing to see where your limitations lie.

A little success is not enough. You have to believe in burning it all down, or you will face burnout. I've talked to so many seemingly successful business owners who are thinking about cashing in. They either feel like their work is no longer a challenge and they've become bored, or the obstacles they're facing are too great and their motivation is too low. If you fall into either category, the solution is the same. You must recommit to a definition of success and purpose that makes you want to get out of bed every morning.

After the forced shutdowns in 2020 and beyond, many small businesses simply never reopened. Some owners figured it was the Universe's way of telling them it was time to retire. Others thought reopening was just too much work, and they lacked motivation to continue.

But others — faced with the same financial hardships and challenges — chose to keep moving forward. What was the difference? Those who continued, despite the challenges and the allure of "retirement," have one thing in common: a greater purpose. Whether it was a printing company that needed to keep its doors open to pay the family's bills or a coffee shop that recognized the critical role it played in the community, business owners who had their eyes set on their home plate were committed to succeeding despite any setbacks.

A few months ago, I was talking to Frank, who owns a custom cabinetry company with his brother. The brothers were determined to blast through the labor shortages, governmental bureaucracy, and supply chain issues that were threatening their business. I asked him why he was so focused on success when a lot of others had regressed to Level Two Retreat.

"What else are we gonna do, Grant?" he asked. "We've got clients counting on us. We've got a big family counting on us. We've got employees counting on us." This responsibility wasn't weighing him down. It was giving him purpose and energizing him.

It was spurring him on to 10X Action.

10X ACTION: GET THE LIGHTER FLUID

If you've ever watched a weight-loss show like *The Biggest Loser*, you'll notice something interesting. As soon as the contestants get off the show, most of them gain back a large amount of weight.[29] In my opinion, the reason is simple. Their purpose was to win a contest. Once that purpose was removed, they had no motivation to keep moving forward and taking Level Four Massive Action. They stagnated, and in some cases, retreated.

This phenomenon occurs in every area of life — fitness, finances, relationships, you name it. Once an initial goal is reached, we have a choice: we can let the fire burn out, or we can add some lighter fluid and burn the place down. Unfortunately, most people choose the former and then wonder why their life has plateaued and they lack motivation.

You must do the opposite. No matter what level of success you achieve, you must continue to build and grow, burning hotter and brighter. Keep taking action until the fire you've built is so big that nothing can stop it. Don't fall into the trap of believing a little success is enough, that one retail outlet, $1 million, $5 million, or even $50 million is enough. Do not settle for less than you can achieve.

And as long as you are alive, you have the potential for more. The finish line will keep moving as your skills, desires, and action expand.

Think about the physical world. Plants grow, or they die. You'll never hear an apple tree say, "Yeah, I've produced enough fruit. I think I'll take a vacation." Likewise, in your own body you're either renewing or you're dying. You couldn't stop creating new cells if you tried. It is when we attempt to stifle this natural process of regeneration that we will feel frustrated, depressed, and "burnt out."

That is why you must continue to push boundaries in your business. You must unleash Massive Action upon your goals and sustain that action. Do not hold back. Do not worry that you'll run out of creativity, ideas, or hours in the day. People ask me how I have so much energy. It's because I do stuff! The more I do, the more I'm inspired to do, all because I am clear on my purpose. There is no other option for me but to continue forward at Level Four Massive Action until I arrive. And when I do, there will be a new destination.

You can never take "too much" action. There is no such thing! Others may try to dissuade you simply because your success and activity make them feel uncomfortable. That is their problem, not yours. Others will ask you to slow down and belittle your efforts because it makes them look bad. Ignore them.

Instead, keep adding wood to the pile, spray the whole thing with lighter fluid, and build a fire so hot and bright that others light their way by it.

CHAPTER RECAP

- Lose sight of your purpose, and you will lose your focus. Lose your focus, and you will lose your edge.
- Rather than sapping your energy and drive, the pursuit of your 10X Success will call forth the best in you and motivate you to toward greater accomplishments.
- To have an extraordinary life, you must continuously push yourself to your edge.
- As long as you are alive, you have the potential for more.
- You're growing, or you're dying. Your business is either growing or dying.

WHAT REALLY IS BURNOUT?

"Existential burnout" sounds like a severe condition, but it's simply a loss of meaning in your daily work."[30] When you aren't able to see the connection between your efforts and their impact, it's easy to lose your motivation.

If that's what's got you down, the answer is clear. When you start feeling depleted, take some Vitamin P (for purpose)!

YOUR TURN

Think of the most **SUCCESSFUL PEOPLE** you know: mentors, idols, people who have inspired you in any field. Are these people who led **"BALANCED" LIVES?** What have other people said about their **PURPOSE** or **PASSION?**

_____
_____
_____

One of the most **POWERFUL TOOLS** you have in your tool chest is **VISUALIZATION** — creating a mental picture of a future state in vivid detail. Spend five minutes picturing your **"WHY"** — the purpose behind what you do that drives you. What will it feel like? Smell like? Sound like? Look like? Taste like? Write out a picture that is so detailed that it pulls you forward to it.

_____
_____
_____

10X My business is either growing, or it's dying.

> "Wake up! No one is coming to save you."
>
> — GC

CHAPTER 10

EXCUSE-FREE LIVING (A.K.A., "DON'T BE A VICTIM")

There's a common narrative in the United States that anyone who's successful has gained their success at the expense of someone else. This is a lie perpetuated by those who seek to destroy the prosperous, who want you to adopt a victim mindset, and whose goal is to make you dependent on the government so they can control you.

This refrain of "financial success is evil" is so pervasive that you must continue to inoculate yourself against it, lest you begin to take it to heart and feel guilty about your ability to create and grow a profitable business.

To fight against the lies being told about you, read the following and repeat as often as necessary:

Don't let anyone make you feel bad about creating financial, business, or personal success. If you have done so ethically, you are a net positive on the world around you. The idea that you should be punished for being successful is twisted. (It's also interesting that often the loudest voices in this critique come from politicians who often have done nothing and created nothing themselves and who DO make it harder to be successful through excessive regulations, red tape, bureaucratic mumbo-jumbo, and taxation.)

In fact, the more successful you are, the more opportunity you provide to others through the jobs you create, through the investments you make in your business, and through the inspiration you provide to others to build their own businesses.

Think about the husband-and-wife owners of a corner mini-mart. They provide not only for their own family, they also employ several cashiers, a delivery person, and a cleaning service. They contribute to the economy through the inventory they purchase, the taxes they pay, and the thousands of other individuals who are involved in the manufacturing and delivery of the products they stock on their shelves. The positive ripples of their business extend far beyond their own pockets. And in running a successful business, they inspire others to do the same.

Despite what others may say, there are no limits to success in the world. Your success as a business owner takes nothing from anyone else. If you are a person of integrity, you are not taking food out of anyone else's mouth, and you are not preventing others from succeeding. Instead, you are making the world a better place through the products and services you provide, the people you employ, and the example you set.

I went on *Undercover Billionaire* in 2020 to counter this claim that the American dream is dead. I wanted to prove that anyone can succeed if they set extraordinary goals and take massive levels of action to achieve those goals — even if they were an unknown person with no financial backing and no reputation. I proved that 10X Mindset coupled with 10X Action will win every time.

So why the campaign against the successful entrepreneur?

People want to demonize you for several reasons. First is pure envy. It is much easier for others to say that you did not get where you are by playing fairly. Somehow you "cheated" and should be punished. But think of it this way. If it is true that anyone can be successful, then those not reaching their goals are falling short because of personal failings, not because the deck is stacked against them. No one wants to admit that they themselves are the problem. It's more comfortable to point fingers and blame. When someone has given up on their own dreams, they want to bring others down as well.

The second reason there's a growing antibusiness sentiment is that the government is interested in self-preservation. If everyone could be independently successful, there would be no reason for the government to exist in its current form and certainly no reason for its expansion. Therefore, they must take what you create and make it seem like you are the problem.

The entrepreneur has to deal with red tape, taxes, regulations, and more. These all make it difficult for an individual to be successful as an entrepreneur.

In our political climate, those who are doing well (despite the barriers put in their way) are vilified and made to help those who are not producing anything or contributing anything. It's a popular social opinion intended to keep the poor, poorer and to make sure that the helpless don't learn how to help themselves. It also penalizes the wealthy, so they are disincentivized to continue to create more wealth.

I cannot tell you how many times I've been told that I am a successful businessperson solely because of my background, my skin color, pure luck, or some other perceived advantage. "You can make money because you *have* money," I'm told. "Not everyone can do what you have done."

By now, I hope you can see that when someone says this to me, it's nothing more than an excuse and a deflection from their own failings.

I was raised without a father and entered my young adulthood with an anger issue, a drug issue, and a chip-on-my-shoulder issue. No family connections. No startup capital. As you may recall, I was told I'd never be more than an addict and should give up on any thoughts of ambition beyond my sobriety.

What I did have, though, was a determination to succeed. I was obsessed with success, and when I combined that obsession with 10X Mindset and 10X Action, I became unbeatable. Once I embraced the idea that nothing happens to me but happens because of me, my life turned around. I realized that no one was coming to save me. If there was to be a hero, a knight in shining armor, it would have to be me. I would need to save myself.

For me, "saving myself" means constantly pushing myself to see what my true capabilities are. That's my definition of success — leaving it all on the playing field, holding nothing back. How big do I want to grow? As big as possible. How many people do I want to impact? All eight billion of them.

Call me greedy, a dirty capitalist, a jerk … I've been called all of these and worse. But the honest truth is that "enough" will never be enough for me, simply because enough is someone else's idea of what I deserve or should have. No one gets to define my limitations but me.

Taking 100 percent responsibility for everything in your life, good and bad, is your path to freedom and to success.

10X MINDSET: SUCCESS IS MANDATORY

No one's gonna show up at your front door and make your dreams come true. When you accept that you must be your own savior, you realize something critical: *Success is no longer optional.* You owe it to the world to spread the word about your business far and wide, and you owe it to yourself and your family to make the most of the opportunities, skills, and abilities you've been given. To do anything less is unethical.

PICK ONE: ☐ **SUCCESS** ☐ **EXCUSES**

Almost nothing makes me more angry than seeing someone with an incredible opportunity to grow their business and help more people decide to "relax and take it easy." It is an insult to your creator and to those who need what your company provides to do anything less than your absolute best to help as many people as possible.

If success is an option rather than a requirement, you will never live to your full potential. If you don't consider it your duty to live up to your potential, if it isn't an ethical issue for you, you simply won't do it. There are too many challenges, obstacles, distractions, and ready-made excuses.

In a previous chapter, I talked about the large number of businesses that chose not to open up after the forced shutdowns of 2020 and 2021. These business owners did not consider the success of their business to be mandatory. Instead, they were distracted by leisure time and challenged by the economic environment, and they found it easier to just quit. As a result, they let down their clients, their communities, their families, and themselves. They redefined "success" to mean relaxation rather than achievement, average rather than extraordinary.

As tempting as it is to say that will never happen to you, if you don't consider it your duty to live up to your potential and create massive amounts of success, you won't. You, too, will fall victim to a lifestyle of comfort and inertia. I know how hard it is to handle employee problems, supplier problems, and customer problems for 16 hours a day and then go to bed at night still thinking about work, only to get up and do it all over again. That's why your purpose (chapter 9) is so critical. You must be driven by an absolute certainty that you cannot live any other way.

Success must become an ethical issue where it becomes more painful to fail than it is to push yourself. Visiting 50 clients in 10 cities in 5 days? No problem. Getting 100 nos from bankers before you find one who says "yes"? Just another day at the office. Selling your house and using the equity to finance business expansion? Of course. You are so dialed in on success that the 10X Actions required to achieve your goals will no longer seem unreasonable to you. There are no longer any excuses that will keep you from acting.

10X ACTION: COMMIT TO AN EXCUSE-FREE LIFE

When's the last time you had less-than-ideal results in one area of your business?

If you're like most entrepreneurs, that's happened about a dozen times in the last hour!

Any business owner can tell you that the question isn't "if" things will go wrong, but "when" things go wrong … because they will. There's an old adage that says a jet from New York to San Francisco spends 90 percent of the trip off course but still lands in the right place at close to the right time. This is an appropriate metaphor because entrepreneurship is largely a matter of course correction.

And I'll tell you from personal experience that course correction is much easier when you take full responsibility for what has occurred. Leave the blame game to the losers. As I say, you can have success, or you can have excuses. You can't have both.

Looking to external forces is a way to pass the blame or responsibility for your failures or lack of performance. When you are looking to point the finger, you're saying, "I'm not in charge here. My actions don't determine the course of my business or my life."

Take the pandemic shutdowns. They were devastating to a large number of businesses, not to mention our entire economy. It was easy to say, "Well, the government said we can't open, so I guess that's that." And that's exactly what many businesses did.

But there were others who took responsibility for the environment in which they were existing. Because these business owners were 100 percent committed to their success, they chose to look at what was possible instead of focusing on what they couldn't do. They made no excuses; they just moved ahead despite the odds.

By definition, these are entrepreneurs because they are willing to take greater than normal financial risks in order to operate their businesses.

Not every business owner made the same decision, but the ones at the top of their game evaluated the situation and then made fast decisions, knowing it's easier to course correct while in motion rather than to start a stalled engine.

In some cases, they laid off staff in order to shift operations in a different direction. In some cases, they doubled down and expanded their core services, seeking to gain ground. In still other cases, they created entirely new revenue streams. In any case, they did not wait for someone to tell them what to do. They did not proceed timidly. They moved forward boldly at Level Four Massive Action, knowing that retreating (Level Two) or doing nothing (Level One) would not save them, and an average amount of action (Level Three) was not an option in these unusual times.

Were they responsible for the pandemic and the government's heavy-handed reaction? No. But they were responsible for their business's condition going into 2020, and they were responsible for how they responded.

There will always be another crisis, another challenge, another unexpected occurrence. And the willingness to be a leader, to risk when others would not, is what will make it inevitable that they will succeed in the end. The reason why successful people seem lucky is that they quit making excuses and instead take action. They take so much action that the law of averages will eventually bless them.

CHAPTER RECAP

- Don't let anyone make you feel bad about creating financial, business, or personal success. You are a net positive in the world.
- There is no limit to success in the world. Your success as a business owner takes nothing from anyone else.
- Taking 100 percent responsibility for everything in your life, good and bad, is your path to freedom and to success.
- Success must become an ethical issue, where it becomes more painful to fail than it is to push yourself.
- The reason why successful people seem lucky is that they quit making excuses and instead take action.

THE WEIGHT OF THE WORLD?

We are born to make a dent in the universe. In fact, the current push to create victims is actually damaging to our mental health.

A survey by Leadership IQ shows that people who believe they have an impact on the world around them are much happier than those who believe they are victims of circumstance. Additionally, survey respondents who felt they had more control over their lives were more likely to be in better health and show lower levels of psychological stress. [31]

EXCUSE-FREE LIVING (A.K.A., "DON'T BE A VICTIM")

YOUR TURN

Think of **SOMETHING NEGATIVE** that happened in your business over the **LAST QUARTER.** Did you lose a supplier, fail to make payroll, or suffer a setback? How can you take **100 PERCENT RESPONSIBILITY** to ensure the same situation doesn't occur again or at least reduce the likelihood of it happening again?

_____
_____
_____
_____

Think you're not one to make excuses? **HERE'S A CHALLENGE: GO 24 HOURS WITHOUT MAKING AN EXCUSE.** If you're late to an appointment, don't say, "Traffic was horrible." Just say, "I apologize for being late. Thank you for waiting." Miss your monthly target? As soon as you start justifying, stop yourself. Instead, ask yourself what specific actions you'll undertake to change things. (Note: Most people can't make it more than an hour or so without justifying, accusing, or excusing. If you slip up, start again!)

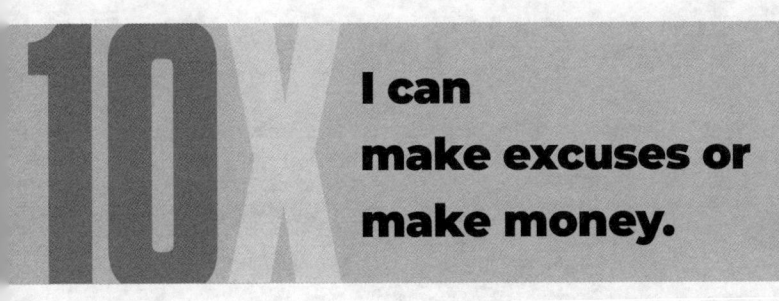

10X — I can make excuses or make money.

> "Luck comes to those who show up and work for it."
>
> – GC

CLOSING

GETTING STARTED WITH 10X

When I think about the final words I want to impart to you, I keep coming back to this: YOU are the one you've been looking for. Heck, you are the one *the world's* been looking for. Things are pretty screwed up. A lot of people are lost and hurting. Systems are failing. The old ways of doing things no longer work. We need **you** at your best.

I've learned over the last three decades of entrepreneurship that I'm at my best when I rise to the challenges in front of me. When I face a problem that seems insurmountable, or I set a goal that everyone else tells me is impossible, I dig deep. My creativity, passion, energy, and drive come to the forefront. I turn off the whiny baby emotions. I silence the voices in my head that say, "It can't be done." I remain 100 percent committed to my vision of success. There is no other alternative. And when there is no other alternative, when success becomes obligatory, things happen.

As we discussed throughout this book, 10X Success for all of us will continue to change and grow over time, and that means you will need to change and grow as well. Just as you are 100 percent committed to reaching your goals, you must be 100 percent committed to your own personal development. The two are a package deal. You cannot have one without the other.

So if personal development is a requirement for success, now I have a question for you: How are you going to become better today than you were yesterday — a better businessperson, a better leader, a better visionary? How will you up your game so you can raise the bar for yourself and everyone around you?

I speak often about how the best investment I ever made was not real estate, my jet, or any physical possession. The best investment I ever made — and continue to make — is in myself. In my 20s, fresh out of rehab and wondering how I was going to survive the next 24 hours without a hit or a drink, I borrowed $3,000 and invested it in a sales training program with tapes and videos.

Those tapes became my best friends, my mentors, my fairy-f'ing-godmother. I listened to them over and over, day after day, filling my ears and mind with knowledge and positive motivation. When I did not have the internal know-how or others in my life to surround myself with, I surrounded myself with the voices on those tapes instead. I absorbed them until they became part of me. Then, I took what I learned and went even further with it. I added my own experiences and thoughts and pushed on.

And now, over three decades later, the information, habits, and skills I learned in those early days are still with me. Every deal I've done, every business I've started, and anything good that has occurred in my life is a direct result of the decision I made to invest in myself at a time when no one else would.

And because my goals continue to grow, so does the need to improve myself and my skills. Training courses, coaches, consultants, experts, books, podcasts … I still invest 10 percent of my time and income on personal development. Why? Because enough ain't ever enough, baby!

It doesn't matter how good I am, I can always become better, and I'm never satisfied. You shouldn't be, either. We're built to strive and push ourselves, and that means pushing our skills and capabilities.

Anyone who's been in business for any length of time knows that there's always something new coming your way. Changes in how to manage and lead teams, new legal regulations, new market opportunities … nothing stays the same, nor should it. So if you're not actively expanding your knowledge and skills, you're gonna get left in the dust.

Entrepreneurs already know this, which is why this group tends to be at the forefront of personal development habits like reading. While the average person won't pick up a single book this year, the average entrepreneur will read 50 or 60.[32] But even that's not enough (unless you want to be "average!").

You must continue to learn and improve your:

- Leadership and management skills
- Processes and systems
- Financial knowledge
- Market knowledge
- Technological understanding
- Communication skills
- Critical thinking and decision-making
- Problem-solving
- And more …

It can be overwhelming, and often you end up focusing on whatever area is causing a pain in your ass at that moment. That's not always the right approach, though. After working with hundreds of businesses and entrepreneurs through our 10X 360 and Business Boot Camps, it's clear that growing a business to $100 million takes a predictable path.

The same things break at the same points in the journey, and the fix is not always what you think it is. Often, you have to go backward in order to move forward. Getting the foundations in place makes everything else a lot simpler. (To find out more about our 10X 360, 10X Business Boot Camps, and our Cardone Ventures programs, visit **GrantCardone.com**.)

Success leaves clues. That doesn't mean it's always easy, but if you continue to up your game, there's no reason you cannot be as successful as you desire.

Think this all sounds expensive and time-consuming when you already have so many pressures and to-do items on your list? I never, ever consider spending money and time on acquiring skills, improving my mindset, or increasing my abilities, as an expense. It is an investment, and it's the only investment I know that can never decrease in value.

10X MINDSET: EMBRACE THE PATH

Successful people simply think differently. They approach challenges and problems differently. They see themselves differently. And they adopt certain habits and characteristics that allow them to pursue 10X Success.

I'm not going to debate whether this perspective was present at birth or assumed sometime later, namely because it's irrelevant. What matters is what you choose to do today.

In one of the final chapters of the original book, *The 10X Rule*, I list thirty-two different characteristics of successful people. Interestingly, many of these habits (Focus on Opportunity, Love Challenges, Seek to

Solve Problems, Take Risks) are inherent in the entrepreneurial mindset. But some may be more challenging for people like you and me, and that's what I want to review here. So here are three mindset shifts to focus on in your quest for 10X Success:

1. **Be Unreasonable.** When you are in pursuit of unreasonable success, you will have to be unreasonable to get there. You will have to set unreasonable goals and then take what many will consider to be unreasonable actions. You will have to work harder than the vast majority of people because you want a life the vast majority of people will never have. You will also make decisions that, on the surface, seem illogical, but somehow in your gut, you know you're right. I faced this when making the decision to buy a private jet. I couldn't make sense of it on paper, but I knew it was the right thing to do ... And it turned out to be one of the best decisions of my life.

2. **Create Wealth.** I would say that a full 90 percent of people are financially illiterate. The number is probably only slightly higher for entrepreneurs. Most of us were all raised with a long list of money myths that are keeping us broke, one of which is the focus on trading time for money rather than creating wealth. I encourage you to re-educate yourself and start thinking in terms of creating wealth, not salaries. Smart business owners invest in their own companies to increase their wealth, not their income. Income is taxed; wealth is not. I am determined to pay zero taxes — legally. You must move your attention toward wealth creation. Stay broke, stay hungry, and stop thinking about "making" money. Create wealth instead.

3. **Be Interested in the Group.** Being an entrepreneur can be a lonely road to walk. Being a 10X Entrepreneur can isolate you

even further. That's why it's essential to belong to a group of people that will lift you up, push you on, and kick you in the ass when you need it. You can only be as successful as the individuals with whom you associate yourself — and the most successful people will want to surround themselves with those who want to bring the entire team to a higher level. Care about those around you. And if you're in the wrong group, find a new one.

10X ACTION: CHOOSE WHO IS ALLOWED TO SPEAK INTO YOUR LIFE

You've heard the adage about you being the composite of the five people you surround yourself with. To some extent, that's true. I can pretty much predict someone's income by looking at their best buddies and how they spend their leisure time. But who we are today is not fixed. As we grow and change, we may find it necessary to upgrade the people we regularly associate with.

If I had to choose whether to surround myself with a bunch of naysayers and critics or spend the rest of my life alone, I'd gladly embrace the solitary life of a hermit. Yes, solitude can be tough, but criticism or "advice" from average people with average lives is a cancer. You must insulate yourself from it at all costs.

Once, many years ago, I was attending a men's event and looked around the room. I realized that while many of them were friendly, funny, and well-intentioned, there wasn't a single person in the room I would have changed places with. None of them — including the workshop leaders — had anything close to what I wanted from life. "Why am I listening to these guys?" I asked myself. Then I removed myself as soon as possible and resolved to take advice only from those doing better than I am. I would no longer entertain victim mentalities, weak-minded, weak-willed colleagues, or those who chose to remain broken and small.

When I was first considering buying my jet, so many people had a lot to say, most of it negative. But the only people whose opinions I sought out were those who, at the time, were more financially successful than I was. The two people I consulted both said, "Grant, do it. It may not make sense on paper, but it was the best decision I ever made." Because they were walking (flying) the path I wanted to tread, I listened to them and ignored the others.

What about family, you might wonder? What do you do with the people who love you but don't "get" what you're doing? Well, I don't go to my barber for advice on how to run my companies, and I don't go to my sister for input on how to negotiate my next deal. It's really that simple to draw a line. You can love them and share the table with them on Thanksgiving, but you don't have to give them a seat in your boardroom.

Just as we are raised with false ideas about money and wealth, we grow up with many misperceptions and outright lies about who has a right to guide our lives. It's natural to want those close to us to approve of what we do and the direction we choose to take our lives, but it is not their decision. No one — I repeat, NO ONE — has the right to tell you what your potential is. Only you know what's in your heart and what you're capable of.

If you don't already have a community of people who believe in your greatness and are also on the 10X path, create one. Allow me to be the first.

CHAPTER RECAP

- The one investment that always pays off is investing in your skills, knowledge, and development.
- If you're not actively expanding your knowledge and skills, you're gonna get left in the dust.
- Successful people simply think differently.
- You must insulate yourself from negativity and small thinking at all costs.
- Create a community of 10X thinkers and doers.

STAY IN TOUCH!

- @grantcardone
- @GrantCardone
- facebook.com/grantcardonefan
- @GrantCardone

Post about your progress (including your challenges and successes!) using the hashtag #10Xentrepreneur

YOUR TURN

Make a list of the people **CLOSEST TO YOU** whom you have allowed to speak into your life, for good or for bad. Circle the ones whose advice is **WORTH LISTENING TO** (Hint: If they've never done what you want to do, don't listen to them!).

_____

_____

_____

_____

How are you going to **INVEST IN YOURSELF** this week? Here are some ideas:

- Check out the on-demand training in Cardone U at **CardoneUniversity.com**
- Watch my videos on YouTube at **youtube.com/GrantCardone**
- Sign up for Business Boot Camp or one of my upcoming live conferences at **GrantCardone.com/events**
- To learn about partnering with us to scale and sell your business, visit Cardone Ventures at **CardoneVentures.com**

Success leaves clues.

ABOUT GRANT CARDONE

As of this printing, star of Discovery Channel's *Undercover Billionaire*, Grant Cardone owns and operates over 15 privately held companies and a private equity real estate firm, Cardone Capital, with a multifamily portfolio of assets under management worth over $5.1 billion. He is the Top Crowdfunder in the world, raising over $847 million in equity via social media. Known internationally as the leading expert on sales, marketing, and scaling businesses, Cardone is a *New York Times* bestselling author of 11 business books, including *The 10X Rule*, which led to Cardone establishing the 10X Global Movement and the 10X Growth Conference, now the largest business and entrepreneur conference in the world. The online business and sales educational platforms he created, Cardone University, serve over 453,000 individuals and Forbes 100 corporate clients throughout the world. Voted the top Marketing Influencer to watch by *Forbes*, Cardone uses his massive 15 million plus following to give back via his Grant Cardone Foundation, a nonprofit organization dedicated to mentoring underserved, at-risk adolescents in financial literacy, especially those without father figures.

GRANTCARDONE.COM

ENDNOTES

1. "Baby Boomers: Incredible numbers are Buying and Selling Businesses (Part 1 of 2)," California Association of Business Brokers, accessed May 23, 2022, https://cabb.org/news/baby-boomers-incredible-numbers-are-buying-and-selling-businesses-part-1-2#:~:text=Retiring%20Boomer%20business%20owners%20will,are%20expected%20to%20change%20hands.
2. Oxford Languages. s.v. "entrepreneur (n.)," accessed May 23, 2022, https://www.google.com/search?q=entrepreneur&rlz=1C5CHFA.
3. "Entrepreneur Demographics and Statistics in the US," Zippia, updated April 18, 2022, https://www.zippia.com/entrepreneur-jobs/demographics/.
4. Dragomir Simovic, "39 Entrepreneur Statistics You Need to Know in 2022," SmallBizGenius, February 25, 2022, https://www.smallbizgenius.net/by-the-numbers/entrepreneur-statistics/#gref.
5. Simovic, "39 Entrepreneur Statistics You Need to Know in 2022."
6. "Entrepreneur Demographics and Statistics in the US."
7. *Merriam-Webster.com Dictionary*, s.v. "success," accessed April 3, 2022, https://www.merriam-webster.com/dictionary/success.
8. Ken Davenport, "How Long Did it Take Facebook to Recoup?" *Ken Davenport* (blog), *Davenport Theatrical Enterprises*, accessed April 12, 2022, https://kendavenport.com/how-long-did-it-take-facebook-to-recoup/#:~:text=It%20took%20five%20years%20for,%2C%20thank%20you%20rising%20costs).
9. Juan Carlos Perez, "Amazon Records First Profitable Year in its History," Computerworld, January 28, 2004, https://www.

computerworld.com/article/2575106/amazon-records-first-profitable-year-in-its-history.html.
10. Nellie Akalp, "Surviving Your First Year as a Small Business Owner," *Forbes*, May 11, 2015, https://www.forbes.com/sites/allbusiness/2015/05/11/surviving-first-year-as-small-business-owner/?sh=e236e328e55e.
11. "Average Definition & Meaning." Dictionary.com. Accessed April 12, 2022. https://www.dictionary.com/browse/average.
12. "SMART Criteria," Wikipedia, accessed April 13, 2022, https://en.wikipedia.org/wiki/SMART_criteria.
13. *Merriam-Webster.com Dictionary*, s.v. "disengage," accessed April 13, 2022, https://www.merriam-webster.com/dictionary/disengage.
14. Jim Harter, "U.S. Employee Engagement Reverts Back to Pre-COVID-19 Levels," Gallup, October 16, 2020, https://www.gallup.com/workplace/321965/employee-engagement-reverts-back-pre-covid-levels.aspx.
15. Adam Grundy, "Nonemployer Statistics and County Business Patterns Data Tell the Full Story," United States Census Bureau, September 18, 2018, https://www.census.gov/library/stories/2018/09/three-fourths-nations-businesses-do-not-have-paid-employees.html.
16. Michael T. Deane, "Top 6 Reasons New Businesses Fail," Investopedia, accessed April 13, 2022, https://www.investopedia.com/financial-edge/1010/top-6-reasons-new-businesses-fail.aspx.
17. Oxford Languages. s.v. "entrepreneur (n.)," accessed May 23, 2022, https://www.google.com/search?q=entrepreneur&rlz=1C5CHFA.
18. J. Hayton and G. Cacciotti, "How Fear Helps (and Hurts) Entrepreneurs," *Harvard Business Review*, accessed April 18 2022, https://hbr.org/2018/04/how-fear-helps-and-hurts-entrepreneurs.
19. Merriam-Webster. (n.d.). *Domination definition & meaning. Merriam-Webster*. Retrieved April 19, 2022, from https://www.merriam-webster.com/dictionary/domination
20. *Merriam-Webster.com Dictionary*, s.v. "obsession," accessed April 26, 2022, https://www.merriam-webster.com/dictionary/obsession.

21 Christine Comaford, "Got Inner Peace? 5 Ways To Get It NOW," *Forbes*, November 7, 2013, https://www.forbes.com/sites/christinecomaford/2012/04/04/got-inner-peace-5-ways-to-get-it-now/.
22 Ruth Simon, "Covid-19's Toll on U.S. Business? 200,000 Extra Closures in Pandemic's First Year," *The Wall Street Journal*, April 16, 2021, https://www.wsj.com/articles/covid-19s-toll-on-u-s-business-200-000-extra-closures-in-pandemics-first-year-11618580619.
23 Karen Weise, "Amazon's Profit Soars 220 Percent as Pandemic Drives Shopping Online," *The New York Times*, April 29, 2021, https://www.nytimes.com/2021/04/29/technology/amazons-profits-triple.html.
24 Alana Semuels, "How the Coronavirus Helped Grow Amazon's Profits and Power," *Time*, July 28, 2020, https://time.com/5870826/amazon-coronavirus-jeff-bezos-congress/.
25 Stephen Mugo Weru, "10 Successful Businesses That Were Started During Economic Downturns," May 4, 2020, https://www.benzinga.com/general/education/20/05/15944325/10-successful-businesses-that-were-started-during-economic-downturns.
26 Alison Doyle, "How Long Should an Employee Stay at a Job?" The Balance Careers, August 12, 2021, https://www.thebalancecareers.com/how-long-should-an-employee-stay-at-a-job-2059796#:~:text=The%20median%20number%20of%20years,to%2034%20is%202.8%20years.
27 Spencer Lee, "Survey Says 77 Percent of Americans Believe They're Underpaid in Current Job," WJET/WFXP/YourErie.com, August 27, 2021, https://www.yourerie.com/news/local-news/survey-says-77-percent-of-americans-believe-theyre-underpaid-in-current-job/.
28 Mark Walker-Ford, *"The 8 Best Social Media Platforms to Market Your Business in 2021 [infographic],"* Social Media Today, February 28, 2021, https://www.socialmediatoday.com/news/the-8-best-social-media-platforms-to-market-your-business-in-2021-infograp/595834/.

29 Helen Kollias, ""Case Study: The Biggest Loser. Is it impossible to sustain weight loss in the long term?" Precision Nutrition, October 29, 2021, https://www.precisionnutrition.com/the-biggest-loser-study#:~:text=Average%20weight%20before%20filming%20The,the%20weight%20they'd%20lost.

30 Genny Ghanimeh, "Understanding Entrepreneurial Burnout (And How to Deal With It)," Entrepreneur, May 12, 2019, https://www.entrepreneur.com/article/333631.

31 "Internal Locus of Control: Definition and Research on its Surprising Impact at Work," Leadership IQ, accessed May 12, 2022, https://www.leadershipiq.com/blogs/leadershipiq/internal-locus-of-control-definition-and-research#:~:text=People%20with%20a%20high%20internal,factors%20outside%20of%20their%20control.

32 Brian Evans, "Most CEOS Read a Book a Week. This Is How You Can Too (According to This Renowned Brain Coach)," Inc.com, June 27, 2017, https://www.inc.com/brian-d-evans/most-ceos-read-a-book-a-week-this-is-how-you-can-too-according-to-this-renowned-.html.

GRANT CARDONE
Sales Training University

Let Grant Cardone be your personal coach

8000+	24/7	GC
Interactive Videos	Unlimited Platform Access	Coaching Team Support

- Master the Art of Business and Commerce
- Fundamentals of Sales
- Become a Master Salesperson
- Understanding Buyer Personalities
- The Perfect Sales Process
- Getting Past the Gate Keeper
- Improving Customer Experience
- Branding and Marketing
- Social Media
- Theory of Closing the Sale
- Master the Art of the Close
- Cold Calling Made Simple
- Handling Incoming Calls
- Internet Conversion
- Prospecting & Networking
- 100 Ways to Stay Motivated
- Personal Finance
- Follow Up Sold Business
- Follow Up Unsold Business
  and many more...

Scan the QR code to start your FREE TRIAL now!

GRANT CARDONE TV

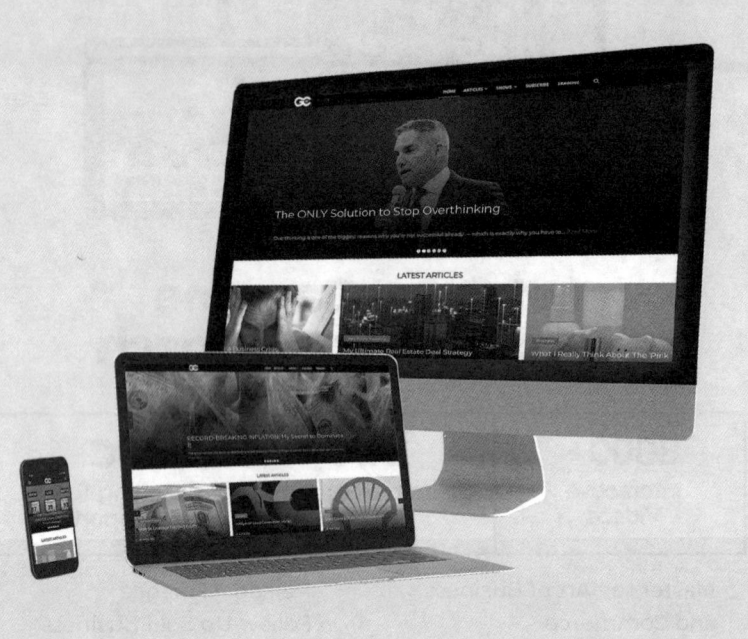

Scan the QR code to subscribe to 10X Daily

This channel is for those that refuse to be spectators and demand to be in control of the content they receive, understanding that the outcomes of life are literally the thoughts that they consume.